TEACHING WHEN YOU HAVE NOTHING LEFT

HOW TO BEAT BURNOUT AND BUILD A CLASSROOM THAT RUNS ITSELF

JENN BREISACHER

Teaching When You Have Nothing Left

How to Beat Burnout and Build a Classroom That Runs Itself

Published by Brass Acre Press, *Wilmington, NC*

ISBN: 979-8-9962169-0-1 (Paperback)

Library of Congress Control Number: 2026914696

First published in the United States of America

To Zach and Carson

Never be afraid to take the road less traveled…if nothing else, it will always leave you with a great story to tell. Love you more.

TABLE OF CONTENTS

INTRODUCTION

You are exhausted.

Not the kind of tired that a good night's sleep can fix. The kind of tired that sits in your bones. The kind where you are working harder than your students, where you are grading at midnight, where you lie awake on Sunday night already counting down to Friday.

We are constantly trying new things as educators, and we should. We should be moving forward, keeping pace with society. Otherwise, we will quickly lose our students because what we are doing no longer aligns with what they see every day. As teachers, we need to stick together. We need to help one another move forward.

You became a teacher to make a difference. To see those aha moments. To be the person who believed in a kid when no one else did.

But lately, it feels like nothing is working. The students seem different. The behavior issues are relentless. The apathy is crushing. You have tried the strategies you learned in training. You have tried calling home, taking away recess, and offering rewards... and still, you are the one going home hoarse and exhausted, wondering if you can keep doing this.

Here is what I need you to hear: *This is not your fault.*

Everything you were trained on was for a different generation of students. The world has changed. The kids have changed. The system has not caught up.

That is where this book comes in.

I am not going to give you a theory. I am not going to give you vague ideas that take hours to figure out. I am going to give you my own classroom trial-and-error, mixed with the trial-and-error of teachers I've helped train around the world since 2018, condensed into practical, actionable strategies that will work with the students in your classroom right now.

You will learn:

- Why student-centered learning is not just a buzzword but the key to getting your students to actually *want* to learn.
- How to give students choice without losing control (or your mind).
- The simple questioning technique that stops learned helplessness in its tracks.
- How to flip your classroom without expensive technology or late-night video editing.
- The one thing you can say tomorrow morning that will change the entire vibe of your room.
- Why "You cannot pour from an empty cup" is not just self-help fluff, but the foundation of sustainable teaching.

This book is not a magic wand. I am not going to promise that every day will be rainbows and butterflies. That is not real. But I can promise that the strategies in these pages are working for teachers right now, in real classrooms with real students. The ones who "don't care." The ones who "never do their work." The ones who "just want to be TikTok famous."

You can tweak these strategies. You can adapt them. You can make them yours.

And you can stop working harder than your students.

You are a good teacher. You would not have picked up this book if you were not. You are just in a difficult season.

Seasons change.

Let's get started.

CHAPTER 1
UNDERSTANDING OUR CURRENT CLASSROOM

If you are like most of the teachers I have worked with over the years, you are trying to figure out how to find what will engage your students and ignite their intrinsic motivation, but everything you try falls short. The student apathy crisis among our students feels like it is getting worse, not better. Requirements from our districts and states seem to change with the wind. EdTech companies pushing products are creating solutions to problems they invented.

We need to cut out the noise, take what is working, tweak it as needed, and get rid of the rest. We need to do what actually helps our students learn.

Here is the reality: Our students have a "scroll" attention span. They have grown up with a smartphone in their pocket. Trying to teach them like we did before that technology existed is going to make everyone frustrated... us because we want them to learn, and them because they hate how we are trying to make it happen.

That is why there is a strong push in education toward a learner-centric model of instruction, which continues to work even today. The problem? There is still almost no guidance about what that actually looks like. Most teachers are left to figure it out on their own and quickly revert to what's comfortable when things feel overwhelming. One behavior issue, one lesson that doesn't go as planned, and it's back to what we've always done (which, spoiler alert, isn't exactly working anymore, is it?)

Student-centered learning, done properly, is not another thing to add to your plate. It is the thing that makes all the other things make sense. It meets students where they actually are. It works with their "scroll" attention span instead of against it, and it takes the pressure off you to be the only one working.

When I first began figuring out how this works, I assumed that if students were doing work and I was not telling them how to do it, then it was student-centered. Maybe you've thought the same and been horrified by what your students would do (or not do) if left to their own devices, without guidance, hand-holding, or the dreaded spoon-feeding of answers.

For the record, that is not student-centered learning. That is just chaos.

Most teachers who balk at this model do so because they think that this is what student-centered learning is all about. I cannot blame them because here is the problem: there is really nothing out there that explains how to do it *properly*.

That's where I come in.

The Five Characteristics of Student-Centered Learning

You might look at an activity and think, "This is great. They are on their own. This must be student-centered learning."

But is it truly student-centered, or are the kids just busy? There is a distinct difference. That difference comes down to five specific characteristics. Just because students are working without direct instruction does not mean it is student-centered. I cannot say that enough. Most articles arguing against student-centered learning rest on this single misunderstanding. They think student-centered means hands-off.

It does not.

Clearing up that misconception is the difference between a classroom that runs itself and one that falls apart.

Characteristic #1: A High Degree of Student Engagement

The keyword here is *engagement*. People often say, "Well, if they are doing work, how in the world would that not be engagement?"

Think about it like reading a book. Sometimes, when you're reading, your mind wanders. You think about something else. Next thing you know, you have to go back and reread what you just read. You physically read it, but you did not understand it. You did not remember it. You had to go back and do it again.

So, were you reading? Yes. But were you reading with engagement? No.

On the flip side, we have all been deep into a good book, getting lost in it. We see ourselves in that scene. We can picture it happening. We are fully engaged in the context, and the outside world feels disconnected.

That is the difference. Are your students just going through the motions, or are they truly immersing themselves in what they are doing? Are they "learning by accident"?

I call it "learning by accident" when student-centered learning is working the way it should. Students engage with the content without even realizing what they are doing. I have seen this happen with my highest performers and my lowest achievers, and so have the teachers I've worked with who have adapted this methodology. It all comes down to how the content is presented.

Here is the key: Engagement does not have to look the same for every student.

I know that makes people pause. "What does that even mean?"

It means this: The idea that everyone should learn the same way is outdated. Different learning styles exist. What works for one student may not work for another, but they all need to master the same information, right?

The question becomes, how do we reach students who seem disinterested in anything new or difficult?

The answer is simpler than you might think. You need an approach that naturally meets students where they are, without requiring you to create thirty different lesson plans. An approach that differentiates for *you*.

That approach is student-centered learning. Let me explain.

Think about trying to teach your students how to dance. You have two students dancing, but chances are, they aren't doing the exact same motions. They are both moving to the beat. They both understand the music. But one might be smooth and controlled while the other is loose and expressive. Two very different styles. Same dance.

Still dancing though, right?

I have seen this play out in real classrooms more times than I can count. My favorite example? My lowest-level history class. The one where others warned me, "Good luck. They will not do a lick of work for you."

With final exams approaching, I needed them to review an entire semester's worth of material. I put them in groups and gave them one task: create a graphic timeline of the ten most important events we had covered all year. That was it. No step-by-step instructions. No templates. Not even a list of the events we covered. Just the prompt and some poster paper.

What happened next was perfection. They dove in. They argued about which events deserved a spot. They flipped through their notes. They debated, compromised, and defended their choices. Groups that normally would not speak to each other were collaborating. Students who had spent the entire semester trying to be invisible were suddenly pointing at the poster and making their case. The class that "would never do any work" worked harder on that timeline than any honors class I ever taught, not because I cracked some secret code, but because I gave them ownership. They decided what mattered. They built something themselves.

That is engagement. Not compliance. Not quiet. Not everyone doing the same thing. It is students finding their own rhythm within the same structure.

Now think about grading. If you are grading the same thing over and over, it gets monotonous. We have all been there. But if all your students are working on a concept and showing the different ways they understand it, it will never get boring.

You are going to see different things that might spark your own interest in the subject in ways you did not think of. They might be showing you concepts and viewpoints you had never considered. There is a lot of learning that happens both from your students to you and from your lessons to them.

That is what a high degree of engagement looks like. It is not about everyone sitting quietly, filling out the same worksheet, at the same speed. It is about everyone being *in* the work. Not just doing it, not just getting through it, but actually thinking, creating, and connecting.

When your students are truly engaged, you will feel the difference. The room will hum. They will argue over content. They will ask questions you did not anticipate. They will show you things you never would have thought of. And you will no longer be the only one working.

That is the goal. Not compliance. Not quiet. Not identical. Engaged.

Characteristic #2: Not Every Student Needs to Be Working on the Same Thing

Another common objection: "I have a lesson plan. I need to stick to it."

I get it. You have a curriculum to cover. Every student needs to learn the same baseline information. How do you have time to get "fancy" with different assignments without making multiple different lesson plans and still getting that baseline understanding of the material?

Here is a thought to have time to make it all fit: flip your classroom. Stick with me here.

In the traditional model, you teach content in class and send homework home to reinforce it. Flip that. Send the baseline information home so they can learn on their own. Then use class time to go deeper.

Why? Because when students get stuck on homework, you are not there to help. When they learn the basics at home, they bring their questions to class. You answer them in real time. Then you build on that foundation together.

And yes... there's a way to still make this work if a student doesn't do their homework!

Flipping your classroom takes some planning. I will not pretend otherwise. I will show you exactly how to make it work later in this book.

Here's the main takeaway from a flip: what students end up doing in the classroom when they are all together should reflect their own learning style. You have visual, auditory, and kinesthetic learners. You probably know right off the bat what type of learner you are. You would come up with different activities to reinforce the material, and students could choose the one that best fits them.

For example, if a student has a strong desire to build things, maybe you can come up with an activity where they can be hands-on, actually crafting something (I can't tell you how much Play-Doh and popsicle sticks I went through in my high school history class). If students are interested in it and know they excel at it, they will dive deeper into the project. They will have a higher level of engagement than if it were something they were not interested in.

That is the beauty of this approach. Students are not all doing the same thing at the same time, but they are all working toward the same learning goal. The objective does not change. The standard does not change. What changes is the path each student takes to get there (because, at the end of the day, the goal is that they all get there, right?).

Some will build. Some will write. Some will draw. Some will talk it out. At the end of the lesson, every single one of them can explain the concept in their own way.

It's all about the journey to get them to that point... and no, this is not more work for you in order to accomplish it!

This is not chaos. This is differentiation actually working the way it's meant to. This is engagement without requiring thirty separate lesson plans. This is student-centered learning doing what it is supposed to do.

Characteristic #3: A Student Should Always Be Able to Tell You Why They Are Doing What They Are Doing

This one is a little tricky.

We have all been there. You plan what you think is an amazing lesson. "They are going to love this! This is going to be great!"

But did you give them enough lead-in to understand *why* they are doing it? You cannot assume the purpose is obvious just because it makes sense to you.

You have been thinking about this lesson for days. You know

the standards. You know the end goal. You know how each activity builds toward the objective. But your students might be walking in cold. They have not been inside your head to understand the progression. To them, a gallery walk might just feel like wandering around the room. Note-taking might just feel like copying words. A video might just feel like a break. To them, it's just another activity unless you teach them otherwise.

That is the key to buy-in. When students know the purpose, three things happen.

First, you can be confident that the outcomes are actually appropriate for your students. If they can explain what they are working toward, you know the lesson is landing where it should.

Second, students take ownership of their learning. When they understand the "why," the task stops being something you are making them do and becomes something they are choosing to do (learning by accident!). That shift changes everything.

Third, you look good during observations. I don't know about you, but in every observation I ever had, my supervisor always asked my students the same question: "What are you doing right now? What are you learning?" When your students can answer that clearly, it reflects well on you.

Here is the deeper reason this matters. When students cannot explain the purpose, they assume there is none, and when they make that assumption, they disengage. Not because they are lazy, but because they are logical. Why would anyone invest energy into something that seems pointless?

Think about it. Have you ever sat through a mandatory training where no one explained why it mattered? Did you lean in or check your phone/grade papers/zone out?

Our students are no different. They are human beings, living the same life that we are.

A student should be able to say something like "I am finishing this assignment because I need to complete it before I can do the scavenger hunt activity" or "We are building structures to understand how difficult Renaissance architecture was to design." Obviously, older students will give more detailed answers and younger students will answer on their own terms, but the goal is the same. You want them to say, "We are doing this for a purpose," not "Because we were told to" or the absolutely dreaded, "I don't know."

Make sure they can do that because when they can map why they're doing what they're doing, you are no longer managing behavior. You are leading learning.

Characteristic #4: There Should Always Be Movement in the Classroom

Gone are the days of the industrial model.

When education first began, the goal was to train students to become compliant citizens. Rows of desks. Sit still. Be quiet. Do exactly what you were told, exactly how you were told to do it. No questions.

That world does not exist anymore. We shouldn't be teaching like it does.

Our students do not need to sit still and be silent for eight hours a day. They need to move. They need choices. They need to be able to stand at a counter, sit on a beanbag, or sprawl on the floor with a clipboard. Some focus better with noise. Some need silence. Some need to fidget. None of that is wrong. When implemented appropriately, it builds momentum in your classroom.

Think about how you work best. Personally, I am most productive sitting back with my legs stretched out, kind of like on a couch. That is my spot. My husband, on the other hand, needs a desk. He has to sit up straight with everything organized just so. Two completely different styles, and neither of us is as productive when forced into the other's setup.

There's actually nothing wrong with that, but looking back, neither one of us was able to explore how we performed best until we were older because of the confines of how we were expected to work. Imagine the benefits for our students if they can learn to do their best work while they're young. Think of the advantage they will have over all of us.

I explained this at a Back-to-School Night once. My room had yoga balls, pillows, standing desks, and regular tables all mixed together. Parents looked confused. So I told them, "Students sign up where they want to work, depending on the activity. They get themselves situated, and the work I get back is better because they are comfortable."

Then one mom had a revelation. She said, "Every day when I get to work, I get my coffee, settle into my seat, turn on my radio, and get myself together before I start. If I need that as an adult, I can only imagine that kids need it too."

She was exactly right.

That made me really happy because that is exactly the purpose of being able to move around. You will get better results from your students when they are comfortable. Not because you made them sit still, but because you let them breathe.

Characteristic #5: The Teacher Is the Biggest Reference Material in the Room

Another notion about student-centered learning is that the teacher kicks back and just hangs out while the students do all the work.

That is absolutely not the case.

The teacher's job in a student-centered classroom is to facilitate. There is a lot of back-end work to make sure you have the activities ready and know where your students are, so you can guide them to where they should go. You are judging how long things should take. If some students finish quickly, you know what else they can do to extend their learning.

All this comes with constant monitoring of your classroom. Whether you have mastery guides or are following online data as your students complete assignments, you are always aware of where your students are. Even though it might look like you are sitting at your computer, you could be analyzing data.

With that data, you determine where the class is going. If they get really into an assignment and need more time to do it right, you automatically adjust to make time. Deadlines, even though they sometimes need to be firm because we all have curriculum to get through, can be wiggled a little to give students more time on something they are really engaged in.

You are literally structuring everything you do based on what you are seeing. If they are not engaging in the activities you have, come up with something they will engage in. Maybe it just needs to be tweaked a little bit. Maybe it needs to be explained differently. Maybe they should work in small groups or move to independent work instead. You have to try to gauge your students to figure out what will work best for them.

If you are not analyzing data, you should be mixed in with your students. Sitting down with them at their desks or on the floor. Asking them questions. As they ask you questions, you should respond with questions or guide them to the answers, rather than just giving them the answers, because the harder they work for it, the more they will understand and remember it. That is what we want. We want our students to *remember* what they are doing, rather than cramming, which a teacher-led classroom often encourages, whether intentional or not.

You should also always be available. Even if you are working with a group or following up on data, you should know what is going on in the room. I always had "help boards" on my walls. A student could write their name if they needed assistance with something, and the people they were working with were also unsure. That way I knew, "Okay, next I need to go over to them." Many times, they just need confidence in knowing where they are.

You are still the biggest reference material in the room. Even though you are not telling them what they need to know, you are still guiding them to find out what they need. And again, this isn't necessarily more work than you're already doing; it's just presented differently.

Think of it this way: you are not stepping back; you are stepping beside them. Instead of being the sole source of information, you become the facilitator of discovery. You are still answering questions, still clarifying misconceptions, still pushing their thinking deeper—you are just doing it in the context of their work instead of from the front of the room.

When students figure something out on their own, with you guiding them along the way, they own it. It sticks in a way that your words never could, no matter how eloquently you delivered them. That shift, from dispenser of knowledge to guide on the side, does not diminish your role. It elevates it, and it turns your classroom into a place where real, lasting learning happens.

Reflection Questions for this chapter...

Think of a student in your classroom who is currently disengaged. What might be underneath that behavior? Could they see the goal as unattainable or unnecessary? What is one way you could test that assumption this week?

I asked my own children how they find new music and realized it was completely different from my own experience. What is one assumption you have made recently about your students' lives outside school? Could you verify that assumption by simply asking them?

How might an anonymous activity like the Baggage Activity change the culture of your classroom? What concerns would you need to address before trying it?

Research shows that disengaged students respond to teachers who allow them to disengage. In what small way might you be unintentionally allowing a student to remain disengaged? What would it look like to hold that student to a higher expectation while also offering more support?

Try This Tomorrow:

Choose one of the five characteristics from this chapter and test it in a single lesson tomorrow:

Characteristic	Try This
High engagement	*Replace one worksheet with a hands-on task or a short video with a discussion*
Differentiated tasks	*Offer two different ways students can show understanding (write, draw, build, or talk)*
Students know the "why"	*Start the lesson by saying, "By the end of today, you will be able to..." and have one student restate it*
Movement	*Let students choose where to sit or stand for fifteen minutes of independent work*
Teacher as facilitator	*Instead of answering a question directly, respond with, "What have you tried so far?"*

After the lesson, jot down one observation. That single note will tell you more about student-centered learning than any workshop summary could.

CHAPTER 2
COMMON MYTHS ABOUT STUDENT-CENTERED LEARNING

That last characteristic from Chapter 1 brings us to a few myths that need busting.

Over the years, I have worked with hundreds of teachers who were convinced these myths were true. Not that they were resistant to change. They had tried student-centered learning the wrong way or had seen someone else try it and fail. The confusion, the misunderstanding, the outright dismissal of the model—all of it came from the same place: a version of student-centered learning that was never going to work.

Here is what I need you to understand: These myths are not based on what happens when student-led learning is done correctly. They are based on what happens when it is rolled out without a plan, without training, and without the systems that make it actually function.

When student-centered learning is implemented properly with clear objectives, structured choice, and a gradual release of responsibility, none of these myths holds up. They simply do not happen. The chaos? That comes from being too hands-off too fast. The lack of learning? That comes from confusing "students working" with "students learning." Is the teacher doing nothing?

That is not student-centered learning. That is just a teacher who stopped teaching.

Let's bust some myths, shall we?

Myth #1: The Teacher Kicks Back and Does Nothing

We just covered why this is not true. The bulk of your work goes into setting up a student-centered classroom in advance so you can engage with the students when you're with them. You are front-loading the effort... planning activities, curating resources, and building systems, but here is the payoff: once it is set, you do not have to reinvent the wheel every year. You tweak. You adjust. You build on what worked and let go of what did not.

You are not doing nothing. You are doing the *right* work.

Myth #2: This Won't Work for *My* Students

There is always someone who says, "Oh no, this will never work. They need structure. They need to sit and be quiet. This absolutely won't work for MY students."

I used to have a colleague who would come into my classroom after school at least once a week. She would ask what we were working on when she walked by earlier in the day. I would always explain it to her, and then like clockwork, she would scoff and tell me that nothing like that would ever work for her students.

We literally taught the exact same kids.

But being honest with you for a moment: there will always be *that* kid. The one you spend all year trying to unlock. Sometimes you will. Sometimes you will not. But you cannot write off an entire method because Bobby is still Bobby. Bobby is like that for everyone. If you can get through to him, great. I have reached students in ways no one else ever could by talking with them one-on-one, finding out what they like, and creating assignments that actually appeal to them. But do not throw out the whole approach because of one kid.

Also, expect pushback at the beginning, especially if your students have never experienced student-centered learning before. At first, they think it is great. Then they realize they actually have to do the work to understand the material. That is when you hear it. "She doesn't even teach. We don't even do anything."

I always laugh when that happens because I know it is coming. I call it the "Student-Centered Stages of Grief." But something always shifts, and you can see it happening when it does. One student buys in. Then another. Then another. By the end, you might still have a couple of holdouts, but most of them get it, and they appreciate it.

This isn't just anecdotal, either. Research supports the benefits of this instructional method. Our current students are engaged, hands-on, and tech-savvy… *when they are interested*. If a student wants to know something, they go to YouTube and find the answer in three minutes. They get what they need and move on, or they dive deeper down the rabbit hole. Either way, they are in control.

We need to meet them there. A model that worked for people with twenty-minute attention spans won't work now. The average attention span is currently measured in seconds. That is a big difference. To boot, a Stanford study found that student-centered learning helps close the opportunity gap (Darling-Hammond, et al., 2014). We all want our students on the same page, but external circumstances often make that impossible. This approach helps close that gap. It keeps students from slipping through the cracks or sleeping in the back of the room. It gets them hands-on and *learning by accident*.

I'll never forget hearing a group of sophomores chatting on the last day of school, ready to break out and enjoy their summer vacation. One of them said loudly enough for me to overhear, “At first it seemed like so much, but then you realize she’s a *really* good history teacher!”

One student said to me, "For the first time ever, when it was exam time, I was not nervous at all. I already knew I knew the information."

I almost cried when she said that.

Another student said, "I have learned more in this class than I ever have in a class before." And another, "Your method of instruction is brilliant." They had never experienced it before. They went through that adjustment phase. They gave it a shot. They realized this is the real deal.

It’s those little moments that make you realize this works, and that is huge. That is why we became teachers. It really does work. It might take some adjusting. It might take some training. But once your students are in it, they are in it to win it.

Myth #3: Students Won't Learn as Much This Way

"If I am not telling them exactly what they need to know, then how are they going to learn it?"

I understand why that mentality exists. You are the expert. You have the degree. You know the material. But being the sage on the stage does not reach every student. You cannot talk at them for forty minutes and expect it all to sink in.

They might memorize it. They might cram it for the test. But do they actually *understand* it?

True understanding does not come from listening. It comes from doing. You can read everything there is to read about riding a bike. That does not mean you can get on one and ride. You have to practice. You have to try, fail, and try again. That is where real learning happens. The same is true in your classroom. When you give students choice, you pique their interest. They become engaged without even realizing it.

Think about what your students know how to do outside your classroom. They can build elaborate worlds in Minecraft. They can edit videos. They can learn a new dance from TikTok in twenty minutes. No one lectured them on how to do these things. They figured it out because they were interested, because they had choice. They were allowed to try, fail, and try again without someone standing over them telling them the "right" way.

The same is true in your classroom. When you give students choice, you pique their interest. They become engaged without even realizing it. They learn by accident.

My favorite example? I had a knock-down, drag-out argument in one of my lower-level classes one day... over *content*. Students defending their interpretations. Challenging each other. Getting genuinely passionate. These were another group of kids that other teachers warned me about ("*Good luck with that group*!"), and they were arguing about history because of how the material was presented to them... and learning by accident.

That is the power of student-centered learning. Not compliance. Not quiet. Engagement that looks like noise and feels like passion. The same kind of engagement they bring to what they care about outside school. We just have to give them a reason to care inside it.

Myth #4: I Don't Have Time to Learn a New Method of Instruction

Maybe you just graduated. You are trying to stay above water. We have all been there.

Maybe you are more seasoned, with retirement on the horizon. You have paperwork, lesson planning, classroom management, and a million other things. You do not have time for one more thing.

I absolutely get it. Nobody has time, and who wants to invest energy in something new that might not even work? Here is the thing, though. You are not being asked to reinvent the wheel. You are being asked to repackage what you already have.

There is not much out there that says, "Here is exactly how to run a student-centered classroom." Most resources just say, "Students should do things on their own," and leave you hanging. They're not suggesting, "Try this," or "If this doesn't work, tweak it this way," or "Here's what worked for other teachers just like you."

I spent five years in my own classroom figuring it out through trial and (a whole lot of) error. Eventually, I found a system that worked consistently for every group of students that walked through my door. Then I started teaching it to other teachers. Together, we have learned what works, what doesn't, what stands the test of time, and what needs to be set aside... and the beauty is, we're still learning.

There is no right or wrong. There is only what works for you. You are not doing new things; you are doing the same things differently, in a way that actually works for the students sitting in your classroom today.

I cannot promise that busting these myths will make every day easy. There will still be hard days, and there will still be students who take longer to come around than you would like. I *can* promise you this: when you stop believing the myths, you free yourself to try something that actually works. You stop holding yourself back because of what you have seen go wrong in someone else's classroom or because you are afraid of losing control. The truth is, you are not giving up control—you are sharing it, thoughtfully and strategically. That is a very different thing. So as you move forward, hold on to this: the chaos, the nothingness, the lack of learning—none of that is student-centered learning done right. What you are about to learn is.

And here is the good news: you do not have to figure it out on your own, as I did. I spent years stumbling through trial and error, wondering if I was doing more harm than good, second-guessing every decision, and learning things the hard way. You do not have to do that. Keep all of this in mind as you go through the rest of this book. Every chapter, every strategy, every hard-won lesson is here so you can skip the years of frustration and go straight to what works. You are learning how your students learn best, and when you put that into practice, they will thank you for it—sometimes with their words, but more often with their engagement, their effort, and their growth.

That is the whole point. Not perfection, but progress. Not a total overhaul overnight, but a steady shift toward a classroom that works for them and for you.

Reflection Questions for this chapter...

Which of the four myths resonated most with you? Have you thought or said something similar? How does this chapter challenge that belief?

I spent five years developing this system. What is one teaching challenge you have stuck with over time? What kept you going?

Think about a time you tried a new strategy, and it flopped. Did you tweak it or scrap it? What would have happened if you had given it another chance?

Which of these myths have you heard repeated most often in your school? Which one have you wondered about yourself? What would it take to run a one-week experiment to test it?

Try This Tomorrow:

Pick one myth that has been holding you back.
Test it. Just for one day.

If You Believed This Myth...	Try This
"The teacher kicks back and does nothing."	*Front-load your prep tonight. Plan one student-centered activity. Tomorrow, facilitate instead of lecturing. Notice how different your work becomes—not absent, just redirected.*
"This won't work for all my students."	*Pick one "hard to reach" student. Design one small choice into tomorrow's lesson. Just one. See what happens. You are not overhauling everything. You are just opening one door.*
"Students won't learn as much this way."	*After tomorrow's lesson, do a quick exit ticket. Ask "What is one thing you understand better now than you did yesterday?" Compare the answers to what you usually see after a lecture. You might surprise yourself.*
"I don't have time to learn a new method."	*Don't learn a new method! Just repackage one lesson you already teach. Take what you have and add one element of choice. That is it. No new lesson plan. No late night. Just a small shift.*

Before you leave tomorrow, jot down one observation. What worked? What felt weird? What would you tweak next time?

CHAPTER 3
UNDERSTANDING STUDENT INTENT

Throughout time, life has thrown society curveballs: The invention of the printing press. The Industrial Revolution. The rise of the internet. Each time, the way things were done changed entirely, and when these massive shifts happened, institutions had one of three outcomes: they adapted and thrived, they clung on and barely survived, or they refused to change and disappeared completely.

We are facing one of those moments right now in education.

Think about the characteristics of student-centered learning: high engagement, differentiation, movement, and the teacher as facilitator. Ten years ago, these might have been considered "nice to have" extras, innovative approaches for progressive classrooms, but not necessities.

That is no longer true. They are survival skills now, not because a consultant said so or because a district administrator mandated it, but because of what is actively happening in our classrooms every day. Our current students learn differently from any generation before them. They are hands-on. They are visual. They need to know the purpose behind what they are doing. They will not sit still for a forty-minute lecture. They will not passively absorb information just because you are the expert in the room.

Their *intent* is different as students. If we do not adapt to that reality, or if we try to teach the same way we were taught (and, in many cases, taught to teach), we will lose them. It's not because we are bad teachers. It's because the world has changed, and we are still trying to teach as if it hasn't. The good news? You get to choose which outcome defines your classroom moving forward. You can thrive. You already have the foundation; now let's build on it.

What IS Student Intent?

Student intent is simply the underlying reason a student engages, or refuses to engage, with what is happening in your classroom. It is the "why" behind the behavior.

There is a very simple misconception about disengagement: *Disengaged students are not lazy.* They are logical. They disengage because doing nothing is easier than working toward something they believe is unattainable or unnecessary. If they don't believe something has merit, they're not going to engage with it, no matter how much you want them to or know they should.

This is the heart of student intent. A student who will not pick up a pencil may be convinced they are too far behind to ever catch up. A student who acts out may have never had a teacher genuinely believe in them. A student who seems apathetic may be the first in their family to even consider graduating. The behavior is not the problem; it's a symptom. The real problem is what the student believes about themselves and their future, and much of that is dictated by the world around them.

Our students and their behavior are a direct reflection of our society.

Student intent is not about compliance. It is not about getting students to do what you say. It is about uncovering what they actually need, even if they do not yet know how to say it, and then giving them a path to get there. When you understand student intent, you stop managing behavior and start leading learning.

What This Means for Your Classroom

Think about the classroom fifty years ago. Rows of desks. Silent students. Compliance over curiosity. It was a different world, and that model worked for that world.

But that world is gone.

Today, our students live surrounded by technology. They will be competing for jobs one day that do not even exist yet. If we are not changing with the times, we are doing them a disservice. We need to prepare them for all of it, not just the content but also the curiosity, the adaptability, and the drive to learn on their own.

That starts with connection. Students who feel connected to their school experience have greater academic success and are more likely to seize opportunities, but I am confident you already know this. You would not be here if that concept were not on your radar, but it is worth saying anyway. The goal of increasing student engagement is not just better test scores or smoother observations. It is helping students feel connected because when that happens, the positive effects ripple far beyond your classroom walls, and it fills your teacher cup to the brim.

How to Find Student Intent

You cannot find student intent by guessing. You cannot rely on your own childhood experiences or assumptions about what "kids these days" care about. I learned this in real time when I asked my own children how they discover new music. It dawned on me that they do not listen to the radio as I did. They laughed. "A friend told me," they said. "Someone showed me a YouTube video." Their musical world is word of mouth and social media. Mine was FM radio. Same concept, completely different delivery.

The same is true in your classroom. You have to ask, and then you have to listen. Below are two interactive ways to do that, but the possibilities are truly endless.

Goal Setting with a Twist

One of the most effective tools I have found is identifying student intent, which is goal-setting with a twist. Have students choose a goal they would like to achieve within a set time frame, such as by the end of the marking period or the school year. Instead of letting them say something generic like, "I want an A" (the easy way out), make them choose something meaningful and pick a feasible reward for achieving it.

The goal does not even have to be school-related. What they choose, and what they ask for as a reward, will tell you everything.

I once had a boy who just wanted a strawberry yogurt if he reached his goal (I could handle getting him that!) Another girl asked me to write her a college recommendation letter if she met hers. Then she changed it to, "Can we just sit down and talk about college? I don't know how any of this works." She wanted to be the first in her family to go to college, but she had no roadmap and didn't know who to ask. I would never have known that without the goal-setting activity.

It helps you learn not only what's important to your students on a personal level, but what they see they're worthy of receiving in return for a job well done.

The Baggage Activity

Another powerful tool is the Baggage Activity. I cannot take original credit for this idea, but when I came across it years ago, I thought it was brilliant. Ask students to write down something that is bothering them, something heavy on their heart, on an unsigned piece of paper. Crumple it. Throw it across the room. Knock the papers around a bit. Have everyone pick up a random one and read it aloud. The writer can claim it or stay silent; there's no pressure to do either.

Either way, you will learn what is actually going on under the facade. You will discover what is bothering them, what is hurting them, and what makes them tick. If nothing else, it helps keep your expectations in check with what is reality for your students. It also helps them feel less alone. There are always themes that emerge with this activity, and even if it ends up being 100 percent anonymous, it helps tap into the students' empathy a bit when they know others are going through tough moments in their lives as well.

Why Student Intent Matters

When you know what your students actually care about, you can stop throwing spaghetti at the wall and start designing lessons that matter to *them*. You can connect the curriculum to their real lives. You can show them that school is not just a place they have to go to, but a place that can help them get to where they already want to be.

Students can see right through busywork, but when they feel a sense of purpose, everything changes. They stop asking, "Why do we have to do this?" because they already know the answer. They stop looking for the easiest way out because the work actually means something to them. They start learning by accident, engaging with content without even realizing it.

Finding student intent takes effort. It takes asking the right questions and actually listening to the answers. It can be as simple as a one-on-one conversation at the end of the day or as complex as a lesson-planned activity. It takes setting aside your assumptions about who your students are and letting them show you. Once you have that information, you are no longer guessing. You are no longer fighting an uphill battle against apathy. You are finally teaching the students who are actually sitting in your classroom, not the ones who were there twenty years ago, and that changes everything.

Finding What Works for You

Try goal-setting activities. Try the Baggage Activity. If you do a quick search, you can find a ton of other similar ideas out there as well. You also know your students best, as well as the culture of your school and community. You can come up with your own ideas, too.

Finding out who the kids are at that base layer is the key to really getting them engaged, excited, and doing things in the classroom.

Just remember that not every activity will land the way you hope, and that is okay. You might try something that works beautifully for one class and falls completely flat in another. That is not a reflection of your teaching. It is a reflection of the reality that every group of students has its own personality, dynamics, and needs. Pay attention to what resonates. Notice which students open up and which ones still hang back. Let that information guide your next move. The goal is not to find one perfect activity. The goal is to build a habit of intentionally getting to know your students, and that looks different from year to year, sometimes from class to class.

Don't let the search for the perfect approach become an excuse to delay starting. You do not need to have it all figured out before you begin. Pick something. Try it this week. Even a small window into who your students are beyond their desks can shift the entire tone of your classroom.

When kids realize you actually see them (not just their test scores or behavior, but them), they start to believe they have a place in your room. Once they believe that, everything else becomes possible. The walls come down. The effort goes up. A kid who was just going through the motions becomes a kid who is actually present, ready to learn, and willing to take a risk because they trust you will meet them where they are.

Reflection Questions for this chapter...

Think of a student in your classroom who is currently disengaged. What might be underneath that behavior? Could they see the goal as unattainable or unnecessary? What is one way you could test that assumption this week?

I asked my own children how they find new music and realized it was completely different from my own experience. What is one assumption you have made recently about your students' lives outside school? Could you verify that assumption by simply asking them?

How might an anonymous activity like the Baggage Activity change the culture of your classroom? What concerns would you need to address before trying it?

Research shows that disengaged students respond to teachers who allow them to disengage. In what small way might you be unintentionally allowing a student to remain disengaged? What would it look like to hold that student to a higher expectation while also offering more support?

Try This Tomorrow:

Choose one of the following strategies to try this week:

What to Try	How to do it
Ask a different question	*Instead of "How was your weekend?" ask "What is one thing you are worried about right now?" (Listen without trying to fix it.)*
Anonymous check-in	*Give each student a sticky note. Ask "What is one thing I should know about you that I do not?" No names. Read them privately.*
Goal setting with a twist	*Have students set a goal for the week. Then ask, "What reward would actually motivate you to reach this goal?" See what they say.*

After trying one of these, jot down one observation. What did you learn that surprised you?

CHAPTER 4
YOUR STUDENT ENGAGEMENT FORMULA

Once you establish student intent, what do you do with that information? You start building your student engagement formula. Think of it as your personal playbook for getting students engaged all day, every day. It is yours. It works in *your* classroom, not the classroom down the hall, not the one in the textbook, not the one you saw online. Yours... and only *you* can decide what works there.

However, plenty of people will try to tell you what will work without ever setting foot in your classroom. Workshop facilitators. Professional development trainers. Even your administrators. They will say, "In your classroom, X, Y, and Z are going to work. You need to try X, Y, and Z."

Look, if someone says, "Give this a try," that is one thing. I do that all the time. "Hey, here is a program. Here is a concept. Give it a shot." That is helpful.

But mandating across the board? That's not it.

Here is the problem with blanket mandates. They assume every teacher, every classroom, and every group of students is the same. They are not. What works beautifully for the teacher down the hall might flop miserably for you... not because you are doing anything wrong, but because your students, your teaching style, and your energy are different.

Say you find a program or system that you cannot stand using, something that does not spark joy in your life. Do not use it. Not because it is a bad program, but because you will not implement it well. You will avoid it. You will go through the motions half-heartedly. No matter how much the kids might like it, if they can tell you are not excited, that energy will eventually trickle down.

I have seen this happen more times than I can count. A teacher is told to adopt a new curriculum or a new classroom management system. They try, they really do, but every time they pull out the materials, they feel a little bit of their soul leave their body. The kids pick up on it immediately. They act out. They tune out. The teacher blames themselves. *I must not be doing it right.* But the problem was never the teacher. The problem was the mismatch.

Here is how to tell the difference between a program worth pushing through and one you should abandon. Ask yourself, *Does this program align with my values as a teacher? Does it fit my natural teaching style? Does it leave room for me to be me?* If the answer is no, let it go. Not every strategy is for every teacher. That does not make you difficult. It makes you self-aware. If the answer is yes, but it is still hard, then push through the discomfort. Change is uncomfortable. Your students will resist at first. That is normal. But if the program fits *you*, the discomfort is temporary. The mismatch is not.

When you are developing your systems and processes, make sure you are just as excited about implementing them as you want your students to be about executing them. That is not selfish. That is strategic. Remember, you are the only person who knows what works for you and your students. Again, notice I said "what works for you" first. Most teachers put their students first without even thinking about it. We are wired that way. But if you never stop to ask yourself, *"What do I need? What energizes me?"* the foundation of your classroom starts to crumble. You cannot pour from an empty cup, and you cannot build a sustainable classroom on a teacher who is running on fumes.

Your Preferences Matter

Keeping that in mind, let's dig into developing your formula. There are three pieces to master:

1. Establishing student intent (you already started this)
2. Determining your preferences
3. Finding a flow

When you bring these three pieces together, you create a formula that works for *your* classroom. Not a script. Not a one-size-fits-all management plan. A living, breathing approach that develops as you evolve your method of instruction. You are not reinventing anything. You are taking everything you already do, everything you have always had, and you are repackaging it. You are not lesson planning any more than you would on a normal day. You are just shifting how you present what you already have.

When you start thinking this way, something shifts. All of a sudden, you realize you have it all together. Not because you added more to your plate, but because you finally stopped carrying what was never yours to carry.

We have already looked at student intent, so let's talk about the second piece: determining your preferences.

You are the engine of your classroom. If you are running on empty, nothing else works. You can have the most perfectly designed student-centered lesson in the world, but if you dread delivering it, your students will feel that dread. They will mirror your energy, or worse, they will check out completely. That is why your preferences matter. Not because you are being selfish, but because an energized teacher is the single most important ingredient in any classroom strategy. Think of it this way: a lesson delivered with genuine enthusiasm by a teacher who loves the material will almost always outperform a perfectly designed lesson delivered by a miserable teacher. Your energy is a resource. Protect it.

I always started the year by telling my students, "I love history, and it's my goal to get you to love it, too." This set the stage for them to at least be intrigued in wondering how exactly I was going to do that. For me and my formula, that was the perfect segue to get started.

To determine your own classroom preferences, ask yourself these questions:

- Do I prefer structure and routine, or do I thrive on spontaneity and flexibility?
- Do I love technology, or does it drain me?
- Do I enjoy working closely with small groups, or do I prefer circulating the whole room?
- What part of my teaching day brings me the most energy? What part drains me?
- Do I need quiet to think, or do I work best in the middle of the action?
- When do I feel most like "me" as a teacher? What am I doing in those moments?

Your answers do not have to be pretty. They just have to be honest.

What to Do with Your Answers

Once you know what energizes you and what drains you, you have a choice. You can either change how you do the draining tasks or stop doing them altogether. Maybe you hate grading at home, so stop doing it. Instead, build in ten minutes at the end of class for students to self-assess. Grade in real-time while they work. Utilize a self-grading program once a week. Shift the responsibility back where it belongs to help your own preferences and classroom flow.

Maybe you love technology, but your students get distracted by screens. Use low-tech choice boards and hands-on stations. Save the screens for the moments that actually need them. Maybe you thrive on small group conversations but feel drained by whole-class discussions. Design more small-group work and let class discussion happen in clusters, then bring one insight from each group to the whole room.

The common thread? You are not eliminating what needs to be done. You are changing *how* it gets done, so it does not drain you, and you can keep up your own momentum. The point is not to force yourself into a mold that does not fit. The point is to build a classroom that fits *you,* because when you are running on your own energy, everything else gets easier. The lesson planning. The grading. The behavior management. Even the burnout.

Your preferences are not a distraction from good teaching. They are the foundation of it.

Finding Your Flow

The third piece is finding a flow that can be both consistent and seemingly effortless.

Flow is what happens when student intent and your preferences come together seamlessly. It is the rhythm of your classroom when everything is working. You are not fighting against your own nature. Your students are not fighting against theirs. Because of this, the learning just... happens.

How do you know when you have found it? You will feel it. The transitions are smooth. Students move from one activity to the next without you having to repeat directions three times. You look at the clock and realize twenty minutes have passed without a single disruption. You are not exhausted at the end of the period. You are energized.

How do you find it? You experiment. Try starting class one way for a week, then another the next. Pay attention to what drains you and what fills you up. Ask your students for feedback. Watch their body language. Adjust.

You might not get it right immediately, and that's okay! Remember, this is a fluid process, and if you don't get it on the first try, that's normal. Take time to reflect. *What went wrong? What felt uncomfortable? What small tweaks can be made to move the process in the direction I was hoping for?* Then you try it. It really is that simple.

Here are a few examples of what flow can look like for the beginning of class in different environments:

- **The structured start.** Begin each day with a five-minute independent warm-up posted on the board. Students know to enter, start working, and raise their hand if they have a question. Use those five minutes to take attendance, check in with individual students, and mentally prepare for the lesson ahead.
- **The collaborative start.** Begin with a quick pair-share question related to yesterday's material. Students turn to a partner, discuss for two minutes, then share out. The energy is high from the first bell, and you feed off that energy for the rest of the period.
- **The choice-driven start.** Post three options on the board: "Review Notes, Work on the Current Project, or Read Ahead." Students choose what they need most that day. Circulate and meet with small groups where your support is most needed.

None of these is "right." They are just options. What works for you might be a combination or something entirely different. It's okay, and encouraged, to mix and match or try something one day and something different the next. You'll determine what needs to change to ensure your flow aligns with both student intent and your preferences, even if it takes a couple of tries.

What if you keep trying and feel like you simply can't find a flow that works? That's okay, too. Again, flow is not something you discover overnight. It emerges as you get to know your students, as they get to know your routines, and as you stop trying to force a model that does not fit. Give yourself permission to try things, fail, and try again. Your student engagement formula is not a document you write once and file away. It is a living, breathing approach to your classroom. It changes as your students change. It adapts as you grow.

Once you have these three pieces in place, you stop wondering if what you are doing is working because you know. Not because someone told you so, but because you can see it. Your students are engaged. Your energy is sustainable. The classroom does not fall apart when you are not the center of it.

When something stops working? You have a framework for fixing it. You do not have to throw out everything and start over. Just go back to the three pieces.

Ask yourself, *have I lost sight of student intent? Am I working against my own preferences again? Has my flow been disrupted?* Identify the weak spot, adjust, and move on.

That is the power of having a formula. It is not a rigid set of rules you must follow forever. It is a diagnostic tool you can use anytime something feels off. It gives you permission to stop guessing and start problem-solving. That, more than anything else, is what will save your sanity in the classroom.

At the end of the day, that is what we are really after: not a perfect classroom, but a sustainable one. A classroom where you are not running on fumes by October. A classroom where the learning does not depend on you being "on" every single second. A classroom where you can trust the systems you have built, adjust them when they need adjusting, and actually enjoy the work you set out to do. That is not a pipe dream. It is what happens when you stop chasing every new trend and start leaning into a framework that works for you and your students.

The next time something feels off, do not panic. You know what to do. Trust the formula. Trust yourself and keep moving forward.

Reflection Questions for this chapter...

Think about a strategy or program you were told to implement but did not enjoy. How did your lack of enthusiasm affect your students? **What would have happened if you had adapted it to fit your preferences instead?**

What is one thing about your teaching style that you have tried to change because someone told you to, but it never felt right? **What would it look like to lean into that preference instead of fighting it?**

"No one else can tell you what is going to work for you and your students." Do you agree with this? **When have you received advice that did not fit your classroom?** How did you handle it?

What is one small change you could make this week to spend less time on something that drains you and more time on something that energizes you? What can you adjust to create more flow more often?

Try This Tomorrow:

This week, try one of the following to start building your engagement formula:

Focus	Try This
Student intent	*Ask three students, "What is one thing you wish we did more of in this class?" Just listen. Do not defend or explain. Write down what they say.*
Your preferences	*At the end of the day, jot down: What part of today felt the most "me"? Do that more tomorrow.*
Finding flow	*Identify one transition during the day that always feels chaotic. Try one small change to smooth it out. Move seats. Change the signal. Add a timer.*

After trying one of these, jot down one observation. What did you learn about your students or about yourself?

CHAPTER 5
CHOOSING CHOICE

Once you figure out your student engagement formula, you'll have the ability to uncover what your students actually care about and how to build a classroom that fits *you* and flows naturally with your content.

Now let's add one of the most powerful tools to that formula: student choice.

Before we go any further, let us get clear on what "student choice" actually means, because there are a lot of opinions floating around from people who have never truly tried it (or didn't implement it properly and had a poor experience). Simply put, student choice is giving your students the ability to decide how they demonstrate their learning. Not *if* they learn it. Not *what* they learn. *How* do they show you they learned it?

That is the heart of student choice. When students have a say in how they demonstrate their learning, two things happen. First, they take greater responsibility for their own learning. Second, you get a clearer picture of what they actually understand, not just what they memorized for the test.

That sense of ownership? It increases engagement. I will say that over and over again.

The entire purpose of this chapter is to help you navigate student choice in your classroom. When I talk about student engagement, student choice is always one of the first things I bring up, yet so many teachers pause me and say, "What does that even mean?" "How does it work?" "I really don't think that will work for *my* students."

I understand the hesitation, but I want to lay out all the reasons why it *will* work and give you ideas you can use right away.

Clearing Up Misconceptions

A lot of misconceptions come up around student choice. People worry about chaos. They worry about losing control. They worry that students will make bad choices.

Let me address that head-on.

We all feel that worry. It is not irrational. You have probably seen students choose the easiest path when given the opportunity.

I hate to be the bearer of bad news, but unless a student is genuinely interested in the content, they will almost always try to find the easiest way out so they can move on to something that matters to them. After all, they're human. Can you honestly say you have never done the bare minimum on something you didn't find productive or meaningful? Even if you thought the task was pointless, the person who assigned it certainly believed it mattered. It's the same thing in your classroom. We cannot expect our students to do as we say and not as we do.

The seemingly daunting part is to combat this in a way that working the system is not an option. Believe it or not, student choice does just that. You are not handing over the keys to the kingdom. You are not saying, "Do whatever you want, whenever you want." You are crafting the activities in advance, setting the boundaries, and deciding what counts as success. The choice you give is within a container *you* designed.

This is the piece I think many teachers miss when they are learning how student choice works. As the teacher, you are still developing the assignments. You are still making sure students are doing the correct content. You are still facilitating everything. But the way you present it to students makes them think they figured it out. "You pick what you like. You do not do what you do not like."

It is like having a toddler. If you say to them, "Do you want to wear your blue coat or your green coat?" they pick one and put it on. It does not matter what color coat they wore. You won the battle of them wearing a coat outside, and they think they won since they got to pick the color. Power struggle eliminated, and what needed to happen, happened. It's the same concept in the classroom.

If you are doing it properly, student choice should not be more work. It should be stuff you already have and are already doing, just presented differently. That worksheet you were going to assign? Now it is one of three options. That group discussion you were going to lead? Now, students choose the question they want to answer. You are not creating from scratch. You are repackaging what you have in a new way to engage your students without a power struggle.

Easy Ideas to Implement Right Away

There are so many ways to add student choice to your classroom. I could probably list a hundred if I sat down and wrote out the different options I've tried or seen other teachers try over the year. Remember, it's all about finding ways for your students to display what they know. On the flip side, it can also be a good way for you to collect data on the knowledge gaps. Here are some examples to help you get the ball rolling (and as with everything else, anything you think would work for your students is fair game to try!).

Questioning Techniques

This takes zero extra effort. Instead of asking, "Does anyone have questions?" (which gets you crickets or bathroom requests), try something different. It may be a simple rephrase to, "What questions do you have?" (It is mind-blowing how that simple shift of grammar makes a huge difference.) You could also try having every student write a question on the board that "someone else" might have asked, or have them turn to a partner and come up with two questions together, or make the process an exit ticket: "Write a question about what we covered today on this Post-it and put it on the doorframe on your way out." The key is shifting from "Do you have questions?" to "Give me a question."

Station Rotations

Station rotations work for every age. I have done them with high school seniors and also personally watched my son's kindergarten teacher do them successfully. You can build choice right in. Let students pick their groups. Let them decide which station to visit next. Offer two activity options at each station, or set a time limit and let them move freely. Within the stations, mix it up: a discussion here, a simulation there, a podcast, or a puzzle. Once you start, you will figure out what excites your students, and the engagement will take off. (See how everything we've looked at so far interconnects?)

Choice Boards

A choice board is a graphic organizer, usually a three-by-three grid, where every activity leads to the same learning outcome, but students get to choose how they get there. You can have them pick one activity, complete a row or column, or play tic-tac-toe. When you use a tic-tac-toe board, put a free space in the middle that says, "Come up with your own assignment." I have never had a student not come up with something amazing. A fashion-loving student once did a deep dive on WWII uniforms. A cooking enthusiast made Civil War soldier rations. The work blew me away.

Choice boards do take a little more upfront planning, but once you have one, you can reuse it for years. Start simple. Let students pick one activity from a small board. Then build from there. The key to creating a choice board is to ensure that, however you have them choose (e.g., three in a row), there is an activity in each potential spot that meets the learning objectives for that assignment. Perhaps each meets a specific standard you need to hit. This takes a little time to do right, but once you get the hang of it, it comes much more easily and quickly.

Remember, you are not reinventing the wheel. You are just repackaging what you already have.

What Success Looks Like

Imagine walking into your classroom and finding that no matter what you give your students, they jump right in. They run to the board to answer questions. They are having arguments over content. They are working together and collaborating to figure things out. The kids are doing the work because they care about it. They are coming up with assignments that blow your mind because you said, "Show me what you have learned." They are making things in Minecraft, on a poster board, or out of paper plates. They are excited about it, and they want to show you. Parents come in and say, "Oh my gosh, he could not wait to get home to tell me about this assignment."

That is what we are working toward.

You have watched them follow the crowd rather than think for themselves. So the fear that this might not work is real. I get it. Learning to make good choices is hard. Most adults still struggle with it. How many times have you made a decision you regretted? How many times have you taken the easy way out when you knew better? Making good choices is a skill, and skills take practice.

That is part of our job as teachers. We are not just teaching content. We are helping kids get better and better at making good choices. That means they will sometimes make bad ones. That is not a sign that student choice is failing. That is a sign that students are practicing a skill they have never been taught. The children in our care are still learning how to navigate decisions. It is up to us to help them figure out how to do the right thing, not by removing choice, but by guiding them through the consequences of their choices in a low-stakes environment.

When you first start implementing student choice, it might not go perfectly. That is okay. That does not mean you throw it out. It means you tweak it. You adjust the assignment. You add more scaffolding. You try again.

That is not failure. That is teaching. We became teachers because we wanted to make a difference. We wanted to light that spark. But somewhere along the way, the pressure to cover the curriculum, to keep them quiet, to maintain control—it buried that vision under a pile of shoulds and have-tos. Student-centered learning digs it back out. It hands the spark back to them and says, "This is yours now. Run with it." Will they stumble? Absolutely. But they will also rise to the occasion in ways you never expected, and those are the moments you will carry with you.

You will remember the kid who never spoke up until you gave him a choice. You will remember the group that took an assignment further than you ever imagined. You will remember the parent who said, "I don't know what you are doing in there, but my child loves your class." Those are the moments that remind you why you started teaching in the first place.

So let them make the bad choice on a small assignment where

the stakes are low, and the lesson is high. Let them learn now, in your room, what happens when they phone it in, so they do not have to learn it later when the cost is far greater. Then guide them back. Show them what a better choice looks like next time. That is not just teaching content. That is teaching life. And that? That is a classroom worth walking into every single day.

Reflection Questions for this chapter...

The "free space" on a tic-tac-toe board often elicits ideas from students the teacher would never have considered. **What is one topic you teach where you would be genuinely curious to see what students come up with?**

Think about the "illusion of control" example with the toddler and the coat. Where in your classroom could you create a similar dynamic, giving students a real choice that still leads to the outcome you need?

Of the three main strategies (questioning techniques, station rotations, and choice boards), which one feels most doable for you right now? What is one small step you could take to try it this week?

The chapter describes student choice as "the ability of students to make decisions about how they are going to show what they know." **How is this different from what you previously thought student choice meant?**

Try This Tomorrow:

Choose one of these zero-preparation strategies to try in your very next lesson:

Strategy	Try This
Change your question	*Instead of "Does anyone have questions?" say, "Write down one question you have about what we just covered."*
This or that	*Give students two ways to respond: "You can write a paragraph OR draw a diagram to show your understanding."*
Pick your problems	*Hand out a worksheet with ten problems. Say, "Pick any five to complete."*
Mini choice board	*Draw a simple 2x2 grid on the board. Label each quadrant with a different way to respond (e.g., "List, Draw, Explain, Act out"). Let students pick one.*

After trying it, jot down one observation. What did your students do that surprised you?

CHAPTER 6
THE FLIPPED CLASSROOM

Earlier, I mentioned flipping your classroom and said we would come back to it. This is the concept I find hardest to get teachers to buy into, which is ironic because everything we do is about getting our students to buy in.

The traditional model of teaching (teacher-led instruction and passive student consumption) is increasingly outdated. It is one-size-fits-all. It does not cater to individual learning styles. It does not foster deep engagement. It does not take student intent or your preferences into consideration. In a flipped classroom, students learn foundational content independently *outside* class. Then they apply what they have learned through active, hands-on activities *during* class time. Teachers curate or create resources for students to review at their own pace before they encounter the content in the classroom.

I know, I know. Stick with me here.

The benefits of a flipped classroom are numerous. First, it allows for personalized learning experiences tailored to individual students' needs. Each student can engage with the material at their own speed. They can pause, rewatch, reread, or relisten as many times as they need. Second, it fosters deeper engagement with the material. Students are not just sitting and listening. They are applying what they have learned in a participatory, collaborative environment once they get to the classroom. Third, it changes the teacher's role. You are no longer standing at the front of the room delivering the same lecture multiple times a day, unsure if it's truly landing with every student. Instead, you are moving around the room, working with small groups, answering questions, and facilitating deeper learning.

Before you cut to the next chapter, please understand that I used to work at a Title I CTE high school, where students looked me in the eye on the first day of school and confidently told me they did NOT do homework... and I still successfully flipped my classroom.

How? Let's look at the process.

Multiple Ways to Deliver Baseline Knowledge

The first step, like all the others, is to find a version of the flip that works for your students. We want them all to move to our in-depth, hands-on activities once they have the same baseline knowledge of the topic. What's the best way to do that? Ask them. Start by giving a technology survey to understand what your students have access to at home. Have them establish backup plans for when things fail (they can't come to school and say, "Oh, well, my internet went down" when they've already mapped out that if there's a problem, they'll go to the neighbor's house). Offer school-based options, such as library time or before-school access. Keep paper backups of any digital content.

Once you know what you're working with in terms of what your class can or cannot do consistently, then you can start planning. There are several ways for students to build baseline knowledge before coming to class. Some use technology, some do not, but all can be effective when matched to your students' needs and your teaching style.

Videos are usually ideal because our students are visual,

tech-savvy, and used to getting information quickly through screens. It's a strong choice because students can pause, rewind, and rewatch. It appeals to visual and auditory learners, and platforms like YouTube make it easy to find and share content. Keep videos short; five to ten minutes is ideal. Use existing content from Crash Course, Khan Academy, or TED-Ed, or create your own screen recordings or narrated slideshows. Add comprehension checks with a simple Google Form. If students cannot watch the videos at home due to internet issues, etc., they can put them on a USB drive and check them out like a library book.

I personally used the platform Edpuzzle when I did my flips. I was able to see exactly where each student was in the process and collect immediate data on their performance on the assignment, so I knew how to move forward with instruction.

- Everyone struggled with Question 3? Let's add an activity that helps strengthen that concept.
- No one had an issue with Question 7? We probably don't have to make that a main focus of instruction moving forward.
- Timmy has had a week and has only watched one minute of a thirteen-minute video? Let's have a quick conversation to make sure he can take care of it before we need to use the information in class.

Readings with purpose work just as well without a screen. Short articles under 500 words, infographics, primary sources, student-written summaries, and even graphic novels or comic strips can be highly engaging. Add guiding questions like "As you read, find three facts that surprised you," or use the CORN method: Comment, Opinion, Reaction, New learning. Have students write a one-sentence summary on an index card and bring it to class. For a no-tech option, print the reading or keep a class set of binders students can check out overnight.

Podcasts and audio recordings are also great, especially for auditory learners. Many students genuinely enjoy podcasts and listen to them on their own time. Find a short ten to fifteen-minute episode on your topic, or record yourself explaining key points you want them to understand. For comprehension, ask students to write down two things they learned and one question they still have, or draw a sketch representing the main idea. If technology is an issue, drop it on a flash drive or put it on a cheap MP3 player students can check out, or simply have them listen during class time as an in-class flip (I'll be getting to that in a minute).

For a zero-prep, zero-tech method, try the "See Something, Say Something" strategy. Assign students to find something related to your upcoming topic in their everyday lives… a news article, a social media post, a conversation they overheard, an advertisement, or something they noticed in a movie or show. They bring that "something" to class, either written down or just remembered, and share it with a partner or small group at the start of class. This works because students connect content to their own lives without even realizing it. They are not passively consuming information; they are actively seeking it.

Sometimes the simplest method is the best. Guided notes or worksheets deliver baseline knowledge effectively when they follow a logical sequence, e.g., ask students to do something (fill in blanks, answer questions, draw diagrams), and end with a clear checkpoint like "I know I am ready for class because..." And instead of saying "Read pages 42-48," try a one-page sheet with three key terms to define, two questions to answer, one sketch or diagram, and a line that says, "The most important thing I learned was... " And always keep paper copies ready.

The In-Class Flip

What if your students do not have reliable access to technology at home? Or what if they simply will not do the work outside class? The in-class flip is the solution. In this model, you move the "at home" portion of the flipped classroom into class time. Students engage with the baseline content, whether through a video, reading, podcast, or guided notes, during the first part of the period. Then they spend the remaining time on hands-on application, group work, or discussion. You are still flipping the model, content first, then application, but you are removing the barrier of "at home" entirely. This ensures every student can engage with the material, regardless of what resources they have outside your classroom.

The in-class flip is often more effective than whole-group instruction because it preserves the core benefit of the flipped model while eliminating the equity gap. In a traditional whole-group lesson, you deliver the same information at the same pace to everyone. Some students get lost. Some get bored. Some check out entirely. But with an in-class flip, students engage with the baseline content at their own speed and, depending on which method you use, you can be actively collecting the data of where they're struggling, etc., so you can move forward accordingly. They can pause, rewatch, reread, or relisten as needed. Then, when they move into the application phase, you are free to circulate, answer questions, and pull small groups for targeted support. You are not the sage on the stage. You are a facilitator moving around the room, meeting students where they actually are (and you have the data to back that up).

Making the in-class flip work does require some planning, but it is flexible. But the core of the model is simple: use the first part of class for independent content delivery, and the rest for active learning. You are still flipping the model. You are just flipping it inside your four walls.

3 Common Concerns & How to Address Them

Many teachers are hesitant to try a flipped classroom because of very real concerns. I know that before I tried a flipped classroom,

I didn't even *want* to try it because it seemed too risky. Putting the ownership of learning in students' hands on their own time, and then requiring that in order to move on, seemed like it just was not going to work. I had kids who didn't do their homework, remember?

However, once I learned how to address these issues when they arose, I fully embraced the model and would not have it any other way.

Concern #1: The Student Just Didn't Do the Work

When you use a flip method that lets you see student completion in real time, you have an idea of where they will be once they enter the classroom. Say you have five students who did not do the assignment. Create a group where they must complete it before moving on to anything else. This helps the high flyers, who often go unnoticed, by giving them extra attention while the others do the grunt work. It generally takes only a couple of times before non-completers start engaging because they want to do the fun activities everyone else is doing.

If they are still struggling to do the work on time and do not seem fazed by the absence of the hands-on part, then you have a student intent issue to address. This is also a relationship-building moment. If a student is repeatedly unprepared, have a serious one-on-one conversation about the issue. In some cases, the student might just be lazy. I had one student who straight-up admitted, "I am lazy, and I do not want to do anything more than I have to." If that is the case, do not give up on them, but know the issue is not as dire as it seems. By completing the flip only in class, they are still getting the baseline knowledge. The hands-on activities are there to deepen understanding. As long as they get the baseline, they are okay in terms of meeting the basic learning goal.

Now, if the hands-on activities are graded, which they often are, you need to take a different approach. The flip can be graded as a stand-alone assignment, so students earn credit for completing it, or you can bundle the flip and the hands-on activity into one grade, meaning they would only get partial credit. Each option has trade-offs.

If you bundle the flip and the hands-on activity into a single grade, students cannot earn full credit if they complete only one part. They must complete both to get the points. This pushes them to engage with the deeper learning, but not always. A student might just take the points for the flip and decide that's enough, which negates the point.

If you grade the flip as a stand-alone assignment, students can earn their points separately. This can motivate reluctant students to actually complete it, because they see an immediate reward. However, if they only complete the flip and not the in-class portion, there might be questions about why they're essentially getting passing homework grades, but zeros on in-class grades. If that's the case, you may need to pivot because, as we know as teachers, optics quickly become everything.

If a student consistently completes the flip but not the hands-on work, have them complete the hands-on activity separately with your support during office hours, lunch, study hall, or before or after school, depending on your building's norms. Usually, it only takes a time or two before they realize they would rather just do the work when everyone else does. Personally, whenever a student did not complete an assignment for me, I had them fill out a paper form explaining why, including the date and their signature. It is much easier to defend the integrity of your teaching method when the student is essentially telling on themselves, and it's easier for all parties to come together to find a solution as opposed to you being stuck defending yourself.

Neither grading option is right or wrong. The best choice depends on your students. If you have a class that needs small wins to build momentum, go with stand-alone flip grades. If you have a class that will do the bare minimum and stop, bundle them together. You can always adjust mid-unit once you see the patterns emerging. The key is to avoid letting one or two students derail the entire class. Your time and attention are resources. Spend them where they will have the most impact. The student who refuses to do the work will not be saved by you standing over their desk. Sometimes, the most compassionate thing you can do is let them sit with the natural consequences of their choices while you pour your energy into the students who are ready to learn.

Concern #2: The Student Didn't Grasp the Material

When you have a way to check what students understood before class, you can tell exactly which students are struggling and with what. This is the power of the flip. You are no longer guessing. You are no longer waiting for test results to tell you what went wrong. You know before the lesson even begins who needs support and where, and can move forward accordingly and almost in real-time.

If any students did not do well on the flip, create a station where they can have one-on-one time with you or a small-group conversation. The delivery method may not have resonated with them. That is fine. You have other options. You can reteach the same concept using a different approach. You can answer their specific questions. You can clear up misconceptions before they become ingrained. The rest of the class moves ahead with the hands-on activity while you pull this small group aside. No one is bored. No one is lost. Everyone is working at their level, and if you do it right, they don't look like they're being pulled aside, but just another group in the classroom working on the next step.

This is all about knowing where your students are when they walk through the door. That is another reason traditional homework is so difficult. In a traditional model, you teach a lesson in class, send students home with homework to practice, and hope for the best. But if they did not understand the lesson, they will either not do the homework at all or struggle through it incorrectly, bringing back more questions than they left with. Then, instead of moving forward, you're spending more time going over what you already have. Either way, you lose time. You have to reteach. You have to correct misunderstandings. You have to cover the same ground twice.

By flipping the classroom, you take out that extra step. Students learn the baseline knowledge on their own, at their own pace, in their own way, and bring what they learned back to you with the questions they have (or that you recognize they have). You are not starting from scratch. You are building on a foundation, and because you checked their understanding before class, you know exactly where to focus your energy. That is not just efficient. That is transformative.

Concern #3: The Student Cheated

When you flip your classroom, cheating becomes surprisingly easy to spot. Here's why. A student who cheated on the flip work will walk into class with perfect scores but no actual understanding. When everyone else starts the hands-on activity, they will flounder. They will not be able to answer basic questions. They will struggle to apply concepts that their "perfect" flip work suggests they should know cold. The disconnect between their scores and their performance is glaring. You will see it immediately.

The key is not just catching the cheating but preventing it in the first place. You want students to say, "It is hard to cheat in your class." That is a badge of honor. It means you have designed assignments that require actual thinking, not just clicking through slides or copying answers from a friend.

So, how do you make cheating difficult? Start with open-ended questions that require personal reflection. Instead of asking "What year did World War II end?" ask "What surprised you most about how World War II affected everyday citizens?" The first question can be Googled in three seconds. The second requires the student to actually engage with the material and form their own thoughts (and if they try, for instance, to AI-generate this answer and you ask them for a follow-up in class, you're going to see it right away).

Next, require students to bring a specific artifact to class.

- A hand-drawn sketch
- A one-sentence summary written by hand in their own words.
- A question they wrote while watching the video.

These artifacts are hard to fake because they come from the student's individual processing of the content. You can tell when something was copied or generated by AI.

Also, mix your delivery methods. Do not always use videos. Sometimes use readings. Sometimes use podcasts. Sometimes use guided notes. If students know the flip is always a video with multiple-choice questions, they will find a way to game the system (remember, they're simply not going to work harder than they have to). If the format changes regularly, they cannot settle into a cheating routine.

Now, what do you do when you catch it? If a student scored 100% on the flip work but is struggling during the hands-on activity, you have a few options.

First, pull them aside for a private conversation. Do not accuse. Just ask. "I noticed your quiz scores were perfect, but you are having trouble with the activity. Can you help me understand what is going on?" Often, they will confess. Sometimes, they will double down. Either way, you now have information.

Second, use this as an opportunity for differentiation. The student who cheated clearly needs to learn the material. Pull them into your small group station. Have them complete the flip work again, or another version of it, this time with your guidance. Frame it not as punishment but as a do-over. "Let us make sure you actually have this down before we move on."

Third, adjust your future assignments. If cheating is becoming a pattern, it is not just a student problem. It is a design problem. Your flip assignments may be too easy to cheat on. Go back to the strategies above. Make them harder to game. The goal is not to become a cheating detective. The goal is to design assignments so compelling and so difficult to fake that cheating is simply not worth the effort.

Making Your In-Class Lessons Engaging

Once you have your objectives in place and students have mastered the baseline content, it is time to design a hands-on activity to deepen their understanding. This is where the real learning happens. The flip delivered the facts. The hands-on activity is where students apply, question, and connect those facts to something real.

Start with application. Do not ask students to simply recall what they learned. Ask them to use it. A math teacher whose students have already learned the basics of percentages at home might have them calculate interest on a fake car loan in class. A history teacher whose students watched a video on the Great Depression might have them analyze photographs from the era and write captions from the perspective of someone living through it. The key is moving from "What did you learn?" to "What can you do with what you learned?"

Next, build in problem-solving. The best hands-on activities have a degree of ambiguity. Do not give step-by-step instructions. Give a goal and let students figure out the path. For example, instead of saying, "Fill out this budget worksheet," say, "You have a monthly income of $2,500. Create a budget that covers all your expenses and allows you to save $200. Show your work." The ambiguity forces them to think rather than just copy.

Finally, add a collaborative element. Students learn more when they have to explain their thinking to someone else. Have them work in pairs or small groups to complete the activity, but build in individual accountability—through a written reflection, a specific role, or a requirement that each person contribute something unique. The social interaction not only deepens learning but also builds the relationships that make your classroom function. The flip delivers the baseline. The hands-on activity delivers the transformation. Do not shortchange either one.

Running a flipped classroom requires thoughtful planning, a variety of delivery methods, and a commitment to meeting your students' diverse needs. It is not always easy. There will be days when the technology does not cooperate, when students show up without having watched the video, or when you wonder whether all the upfront work is actually paying off. But the benefits are well worth the effort, and once you find your rhythm, you will wonder how you ever taught any other way.

The flipped classroom empowers students to take ownership of their learning. Instead of passively receiving information, they arrive ready to dive in, ask questions, and apply what they have learned. It fosters a dynamic and engaging classroom environment where you are no longer racing through a lecture, hoping something sticks. You are moving through the room, having real conversations, catching misconceptions before they take root, and giving every student what they need in the moment. Ultimately, it transforms education for the better—not because it is trendy, but because it puts the work of learning back where it belongs: in the hands of the students, with you right there to guide them.

The flip doesn't just change things for the students. It changes things for you, too. You stop feeling like a performer who has to be "on" every second of the class period. You stop repeating the same instructions five times because half the room was not listening. You stop taking home piles of work that you never had time to address during class. Instead, the heavy lifting happens with you in the room, where you can actually see who is getting it and who is not. That means less grading in isolation, fewer surprises on test day, and more of those lightbulb moments that made you want to teach in the first place.

Reflection Questions for this chapter...

"Being a teacher that is hard to cheat on is a badge of honor." How could you design flipped assignments that make cheating difficult or pointless?

The "See Something, Say Something" strategy requires zero prep and zero technology. What topic could you try this with next week?

The chapter offers seven different ways for students to get baseline knowledge. Which two or three seem most feasible for your classroom right now?

The chapter describes handling students who "just did not do the work" by having them complete it before joining fun activities. How might this strategy work in your classroom?

Try This Tomorrow:

Choose one of these small steps to begin exploring the flipped classroom model:

Step	Try This
Find one video or reading	*Locate a short video or article on a topic you are about to teach. Test it yourself first.*
Create a guided notes sheet	*Design a one-page sheet with key terms, questions, and a sketch box. Use it as the "flipped" portion.*
Try "See Something, Say Something"	*Tell students: "Tomorrow, bring in one thing you noticed related to [topic]." No tech required.*
Flip one lesson	*Instead of lecturing, have students engage with baseline content first. Then go straight to a hands-on activity.*
Send a technology survey	*Find out what devices and internet access your students actually have at home and determine a "backup plan" if they fail.*

After trying one of these, jot down one observation. What worked? What would you adjust next time?

CHAPTER 7
PROBLEM-SOLVING IN THE STUDENT-CENTERED CLASSROOM

Even with a student-centered classroom, not every day is going to be perfect.

Even though the number of disruptions, behavior issues, and engagement problems will be dramatically reduced, problems will still pop up.

At the end of the day, we are dealing with children. Not every day is going to be perfect. Sometimes you will have the perfect lesson planned out, but part of it will flop, or the kids will not be paying attention because of something outside your control. There are many variables, and as teachers, we know we have to roll with it.

A common question in teaching is about student engagement. You give students what they need to do and expect them to do it. Many people are concerned that if you are not standing there holding their hand, they will not get the work done.

That is not the case, but you have to set it up so that it is not the case.

Let me share an example from my own workshops. When I run in-person training, I split teachers into three groups based on learning styles: visual, auditory, and tactile. I give them the instructions for what they need to do at their station. Then I walk away. I do this on purpose.

When they start their activities, they are a little bit confused. I am not giving step-by-step instructions. I say, "Here are the directions. Now get going." It usually takes a couple of minutes of awkward silence until somebody in each group steps up and says, "Okay, let's figure this out," and then they piece it together. When I bring everybody back together, the first thing I ask is, "So, how did that start out?" Nobody ever wants to answer because nobody wants to hurt my feelings. But when I tell them I am expecting negative feedback, they open up.

"It was confusing." "I was distracted." "I did not know what to do."

Then I tell them that this is what happens when you first start student-centered learning, especially if the kids have never been exposed to it before. It is to be expected if you don't gradually show them how the process works and what the expectations are. Might you have a class where certain students step up as the teachers did? Maybe, but chances are you're going to have disengagement and behavior issues, and you'll immediately think, *See? This doesn't work.*

Once they are used to the process and understand how it is executed, only then can you drop an assignment in their lap and expect them to jump right in.

The Gradual Release of Responsibility

When a teacher says that student-led learning doesn't work in their classroom, the issue is almost always that the teacher jumped right in with their very first assignment and was too hands-off, just as I demonstrate in my workshops. It is a gradual process to get your students on board. You do need to hold their hands a little bit more in the beginning. By the end, it is a well-oiled machine. You could throw anything at them, and they will just start working because that is the routine.

I can do that in a workshop in one lesson, because adults figure it out a bit more quickly than children do. But doing that shows them that, by the end, everybody got it together. They see that when I designed those workshops, all three groups got the exact same information, just in different ways. They all knew the answers. It just took them a minute to get there.

In essence, I have them demonstrate the entire execution of student-centered learning in just one workshop, without them even realizing it. I have the adults learning by accident.

It's just important to remember that not every child is going to jump on board and understand right away. There is a tipping point that sometimes takes a couple of days or a couple of weeks, but they do get there.

With student-centered learning, you want to keep the kids on the edge of their seats, wondering what you are going to do next, but not in a "gotcha" way. What I am going to share next is how I used to set up every single one of my classes to eliminate that surprise factor. I did teach high school, but you can change and amend all of these for whatever grade you teach. I've seen it work beautifully in elementary and middle school classrooms as well.

The Daily Routine

Every day, when my students arrived in class, I would give them a daily plan. Most of the time, it was a half piece of paper I had printed out. The daily plan showed:

- What tasks had to be completed that day
- Optional assignments (for students who finished early)
- Any announcements or notes I wanted them to have

If a student got done early, they had other things to do, but if they just got by in the nick of time, it didn't matter if those optional things weren't finished.

Each student had a magnetic name tag that lived on one of the whiteboards in my classroom. I printed them on different colored paper by class, laminated them, and attached a magnet to the back with hot glue. It wasn't much, but it made my life so much easier. When students walked in, they would grab their name and move it on the board. I had each period in a box separated into two sections. They would move their tag from one section to the other, so when I went to do Attendance, I could see which names remained untouched, do a quick scan of the room to make sure it was accurate, and Attendance was done.

Every day, I put the tasks at hand on another board, organized by column. Once everyone got settled and Attendance was taken care of, students would move their name to whichever assignment they were currently working on. This helped me stay organized, see where students were with finishing assignments, and know who I needed to talk to.

If they finished early, they could submit their name to the "Help Wanted" section. That meant that if I was helping other students and was unavailable or if someone just had a quick question, they knew they could ask those students for help because they were already done with their work. This was not about copying answers. It was about getting a quick question answered. "Hey, Susie, can you help me with this?" Students knew who in the room could help, which gave them autonomy.

The Unit Schedule

On the first day of every unit, I would give out a schedule. It included every day we had planned for that unit, the topic for each day, and the essential question students should be able to answer by the end of the lesson. I always included a note that the schedule was subject to change because snow days, fire drills, and anything else can happen. At the bottom, I listed important dates for that unit, and I always told them on the first day exactly when the test would be. No surprises. They knew from Day 1 how much time they had to prepare, which took away the anxiety of the unknown and put the responsibility on them to plan ahead.

On the back of the schedule, I put the assessment study guide. Even when I moved to a more project-based model and traditional tests went away, they still needed to know those key concepts to do well on their projects and assignments. They could look the terms over at home each night, see which ones we had covered that day, and jot down notes as we went. By the time the project rolled around, they had already been reviewing for weeks without even realizing it.

I posted the schedule on my website, on the board, and kept extra copies in the classroom. They could never say they didn't know. Of course, some still did, but then a couple of other kids would always chime in and tell them where to find the information, and I didn't have to be the one to say it. That small shift of students holding each other accountable saved me so much energy over the course of the year.

The Assignment Schedule

Another tool I would hand out on the first day of a unit was an assignment schedule that outlined everything I planned for students to complete. Along the top were the dates the unit would cover. Down the side were the assignments. If you looked across the grid, you could see how many days students had to work on each assignment.

For example, Assignment 1 (a worksheet) had two days and had to be done by the end of class on the second day. Assignment 2 (a reading) could start on the first day, but had to be done by the end of the third day. Assignment 5 (a simulation) had just one day allotted, which meant it was a whole-class activity that everyone needed to work on at the same time. All assignments before that point had to be completed in order to fully understand that activity.

Some assignments were interchangeable. You did not have to finish Assignment 1 to understand Assignment 2, so if a student thought Assignment 2 sounded more interesting, they could start there first, as long as Assignment 1 was done by its deadline. This helped keep students organized, especially those who needed more structure, including students with IEPs. I called this "Unstructured Structure." They had free rein over *when* they did the assignments, but everything had to be done within a specific window. It also helped them learn to budget their time, and I could help them with that individually along the way.

The Digital Calendar

I also maintained an online, real-time digital due date calendar using Google Sites. I had a welcome video and a QR code to our classroom Twitter account on there as well. At the top, I listed my different classes, and I added due dates to their calendars as they came up. If you teach a grade where students already have phones (or even if only their parents have phones), they could sign up for alerts and receive automatic notifications when new assignments are posted or when others change. This was very easy to set up and absolutely invaluable for my students.

Daily Check-Ins for Projects

If students were all working on the same project (not a choice project), I used a similar structure for scheduling how it needed to play out. I would say, "We need four days to get things taken care of. On Day 1, you need to complete this. On Day 2, you need to complete that."

I awarded points for classwork every day. When there were about 10 minutes left in class, I would walk around to each student to see what they had completed. If they were done, they got full points. If they had been goofing off or were not finished, they did not get full points. If they were working hard, or had been struggling, or something happened, and they talked to me, sometimes I would say, "Bring me this sheet tomorrow, and I will grade it at the beginning of class."

There is still room to be flexible on a case-by-case basis, but do not let them think they can ask for extensions whenever they want. This goes for all the assignments you are working through. If you reach a point where everyone is working really hard, you can always adjust your schedule. It is easy enough to say, "You know what, everybody? You can have a little bit of extra time tomorrow to wrap this up." You have that ability. You are the teacher.

I would not suggest telling them about the flexibility ahead of time because we know kids will try to work the system, but it is certainly something you always have at your disposal. It keeps them accountable without making them feel like the system is rigged against them. And that balance, that structure with a human touch, is exactly what makes this work.

Remembering YOUR Growth Mindset

We talk a lot about a growth mindset with our students. I had a poster hanging in my classroom that said, "Mistakes are proof that you are trying." We have to remember that, as humans ourselves, we need to live it too. When you try a new method in your classroom, it probably will not work perfectly the first time. That is not a sign of failure. It is a sign that you are learning. You can tweak it on the fly. Change out a section. Add something new. Take something away. That is the beauty of all of this. Nothing is permanent, and everything can be adjusted.

If the first time you try something, it doesn't go as planned, don't scrap the whole idea. Do not retreat back to what is comfortable just because it is familiar. You need to be willing to work on the fly. That is what so much of teaching is anyway. When you model a growth mindset in front of your students, and they see you try, fail, adjust, and try again, you give them permission to do the same. You show them that learning is messy, that struggle is normal, and that mistakes are not endings. They are just data. You will also discover something else. When you are open and flexible, you become more attuned to your students. You will notice who needs more time and who is ready to move on. You will have the conversations that lead to breakthroughs. The classroom starts to differentiate itself naturally.

That is not just teaching; it's leading. The teachers who succeed with this shift are not the ones who get it right on the first try. They are the ones who refuse to let perfect be the enemy of better. They are the ones who walk in the next day and say to their students, "Okay, that didn't work the way I hoped. Here is what I am going to do differently today." That kind of honesty is disarming. It catches students off guard in the best way. They are not used to adults admitting they missed the mark, and when they see you do it, something shifts. You stop being the judge at the front of the room and become a partner in learning. That is when the real magic happens. That is when the walls come down, and the work gets real.

So the next time a lesson flops, take a breath. Look at your students. Tell them what you are going to change. Then watch what happens. You might be surprised to find it becomes one of the most powerful lessons you teach all year—because at the end of the day, we are not just teaching content. We are teaching human beings how to navigate a world that will not always give them a clear path.

The best way to teach that is to live it right in front of them.

When they see you handle a flop with honesty instead of defensiveness, they learn something they will carry long after they forget the content. They learn that struggle is not shameful. They learn that the person in charge does not have to have all the answers. They learn that real strength is not about getting everything right—it is about having the humility to say, "That didn't work," and the resilience to try again.

Reflection Questions for this chapter...

I emphasize a "gradual release of responsibility." On a scale of 1 to 10, how hands-off are you right now? **What would it look like to dial it back a notch?**

The Help Wanted board allowed students to help each other without copying answers. **How could you create a similar system?** What would need to be in place for it to work?

The Mastery Schedule gives students windows of time rather than strict daily deadlines. **How might this change the dynamic in your classroom?** What concerns would you need to address?

The chapter ends with a reminder about growth mindset for teachers. Think of a recent lesson that did not go as planned. **What did you learn from it?** What will you tweak next time?

Try This Tomorrow:

Choose one of these organizational strategies to try:

Strategy	Try This
Share the unit schedule	*On the first day of your next unit, give students a one-page schedule with topics, essential questions, and the test date.*
Create a daily plan board	*Post each day's tasks, required work, and optional early finisher activities where all students can see them.*
Try a Help Wanted board	*Use sticky notes or magnets. Have students signal when they are available to help peers with quick questions.*
Give a mastery schedule	*For a short unit (1–2 weeks), list assignments and the window of time students have to complete each one. Let them choose the order.*

After trying one of these, jot down one observation. What changed? What would you adjust next time?

CHAPTER 8
REVERSING STUDENT APATHY

If the ideas in this book so far have gotten you the tiniest bit excited (even if it's just a little), there may still be some underlying doubt that they will actually move the needle in your situation.

Tell me if this sounds like you:

You are putting your heart and soul on the line every day, but it feels like nothing is working. You have stopped doing much besides watching old reruns or doomscrolling in hopes of regaining energy and motivation, and it rarely works. With the Sunday Scaries carrying over to every day of the week, you may even be considering leaving the profession you dreamed about your entire life. I bet you have found yourself working harder than your students, pressing through the curriculum even though it is constantly derailed, and throwing spaghetti at the wall in hopes that something sticks.

You are not alone. I have talked to hundreds of teachers who feel exactly the same way. Here is what I need you to hear: This is not your fault. The saying "You can't fix what you do not know is broken" applies perfectly here. We were all trained with strategies that worked *before* the student apathy crisis was in full effect (*I'll get to that in a minute*). That lack of updated knowledge is impacting our classrooms, but it is not a personal failure. It is a system that has not caught up to the challenges we are facing right now.

We have this mentality in teaching that once the train leaves the station, it is nearly impossible to stop it or change course. I get that many teachers stick to tradition because that is what we were taught. Those methods used to work just fine. It is not your fault that you are teaching the way you know how; the world and students have changed a lot. What might have been a home run before might be striking you out at the plate now.

Thinking that a standard traditional lesson plan that used to work will succeed in today's classroom is the equivalent of expecting a new textbook to make the *New York Times* bestseller list. Yes, it is full of great information, but that alone won't compel anyone to read the entire thing or recommend it to their friends. They can just watch a YouTube video.

This is the same concept as using old methods in our modern-day classroom. Realizing that our usual ways might not be working is hard, but we have to be open to new ways of thinking. The good news is these adjustments really help. They are working for teachers right now, and they can work for you, too.

What Students Are Actually Saying

When I was researching student apathy, I read a comment from a teacher about a real discussion they had with their ninth-grade students about why they are disengaged, why they do not complete assignments, and why so many of them do not care about failing.[1]

Their answers were honest and eye-opening.

Many of them simply do not see the value in school. They

1. To check out my research on the Student Apathy Crisis, visit studentcenteredworld.com/student-apathy

feel like they are constantly reprimanded for reasons they do not understand and feel that teachers genuinely do not care about them because of it. In their own ninth-grade way, they were saying that it truly seems like compliance in school is more important than mastery. There is definitely a balance between the two, but the most common reason they gave for disengagement was that they see no point in school. They believe that they can make money through social media platforms or as video game streamers. Even when that teacher pointed out that only a small number of people make serious money this way, most students felt it was a better option than going into debt for college and a job they do not want, cannot get, or that does not pay them enough.

As adults, many look at these aspirations as ridiculous... but how many people do you know who actually grew up to be an astronaut or the president of the United States? These modern-day goals are no different than any other generation's goals, but to potentially make it in the social media field does not require extensive schooling. That is a big difference from the lofty career aspirations of the past.

Let us take it one step further for those kids who do end up pursuing higher education. I saw a story of a professor who, at the beginning of each semester, assigns students a task to explain why they are in college *at that moment*. They are asked why they did not choose to start later, take a gap year, or pursue a different path. The question basically makes them justify their decision to attend college. The responses he gets are fairly consistent. Only about 10 percent of students say they are there to learn. Another 10 to 15 percent mention they need their major for a specific career. Some students are surprised by the question and admit they have never thought about it before, but many feel they are in college because of pressure from parents, societal expectations, or simply because it is the expected path.

We need to make this conversation loud because the world of education, as we know it, is changing. Since the COVID-19 pandemic, many young people have experienced significant stress and instability. This experience has shifted their values and priorities.

If teachers and academics do not adapt to these changes, students will continue to view education as just another task to complete, without recognizing its real value. They will see it as something they *have to* do rather than something that *benefits* them, leading to a lack of genuine engagement.

I know so many teachers dig their heels in at statements like that because the mentality is, "You are there to teach, not entertain." That is absolutely correct. Your classroom is not a theater, and you should not be performing or working harder at it than your students. Engaging students does not mean sacrificing educational integrity for entertainment. It is about finding the sweet spot by incorporating elements that make your lessons more relatable and relevant, and silently encouraging active participation and deeper learning. It is the little things that ignite intrinsic motivation. This enhances student engagement and reinvigorates your passion for teaching.

The Lawnmower Problem

Imagine you have an old lawnmower. You have been using it every summer for years. It always started up without a hitch. But suddenly, it will not start. Do you keep yanking on the starter cord the same old way, hoping for a different result? Or do you start troubleshooting? Checking the fuel, the spark plugs, adjusting the carburetor, or maybe consulting a video for help? Maybe you ask someone else to take a look at it, but you keep at it until the mower runs again or you realize it is time for a new one.

You would not just keep pulling the starter cord endlessly or give up on mowing your lawn altogether, right?

This kind of practical problem-solving is standard in

everyday life. We all do it, but generally, we do not apply it the same way in the classroom. There is a reluctance to do so, rooted in the collective belief that if things were a certain way for so long, we should expect them to revert to that state at some point. If that were happening, we would not be several years into this problem with the appearance of it getting worse. Simply put, we need to start checking the spark plugs and carburetors in our classroom.

I have spoken with so many teachers who feel they have tried it all, but nothing is working. They feel stuck and are at a loss. However, as I have been told many times, if you feel stuck, it is because you have stopped growing. In our teaching lives, that is not your fault. There is a very high chance that you have been trying old techniques, even if they are new to you, that are not resonating with your audience. Think of it this way: If something does not interest you personally, how long can you sit and pay full, unwavering attention? Again, when was the last time you hung on every word at a faculty meeting and had no side conversations, did not grade papers, and just took diligent notes? Just because the person giving the presentation thinks it is important does not mean it feels vital to you... and you are an adult with a longer attention span.

Think about our kids. The ones with naturally shorter attention spans. Do you see what I am getting at?

Why We Stay Stuck

Teaching is a trial-by-fire profession where, most days, we are flying the plane as we build it. When you are in the thick of everything, you just want it to be fixed. "Tell me what I need to do so I can keep doing my job." When you rely solely on practices that worked in the past, you miss out on new ideas that are actually working. Education is constantly evolving. By resisting that, you may find yourself feeling stagnant and frustrated.

Staying stuck often stems from:

1. A fear of change
2. A belief that new methods will not work
3. A belief that it is all the same thing with a new name

This is our subconscious speaking to us. Our subconscious makes us stick to what we know because it feels safer. The truth is, everything we were trained in was *before* this student apathy crisis. A lot of it is not relevant to what will engage your students today. Our training is for the Millennial generation at best, and the last of the Millennials graduated high school in 2014.

If we could tap into just 1 percent of our students' intrinsic motivation each day, think of how far that would take us by the end of a school year. We can slowly build their interest and involvement. It is about small, consistent efforts that accumulate over time. This is not about a dramatic overhaul overnight. You are not trying to fix it all at once. You are trying to fix it one at a time. If you could spark just one part of one student's intrinsic motivation, lean into it and add to it slowly, it will build over time, and it will happen student by student. Remember: You need to win over one student at a time, not everybody at once.

Finding Tangible Solutions

This is normally the part of the process where teachers understand the concepts I've been discussing and start to visualize them in their own classrooms, but they get stuck on tangible solutions to the problems they're facing.

I have found there are five apathy-based issues we see in the classroom, and I'd like to share one action you can implement right away to start working on each.

The Problem: The Utter Fear of Failure

This is not necessarily new, but it is absolutely running rampant. You may have been looking at the strategies I've talked about and thought, *But they do not even care if they fail.* As a whole, it is easier for a student to accept that they failed because they did not put in the effort than to accept that they failed because they *failed.* They are missing the soft skills of brushing themselves off and trying again. With so much emphasis on testing and a society that splashes perfection all over the internet, our kids really think a stumble is the end of the world.

The Action: Teach Them the Meaning of Aloha

I can feel you scrunching up your face. "What does the Hawaiian word for hello and goodbye have to do with anything?"

The best tour guide we had while honeymooning in 2009.

In 2009, I learned that is not what *Aloha* actually means.

I went to Hawaii on my honeymoon. At Pearl Harbor, we had an elderly Hawaiian man as our guide. He told us the true meaning of *Aloha*. In their culture, it basically means leave all your garbage behind. When people would enter Hawaii, they would say, "*Aloha*—Welcome. You are starting fresh. Leave your garbage behind." When those people would leave, again, they would say, "*Aloha*," meaning "You are going to a new place. Leave all your garbage behind."

Even if this is actually nothing more than his own family lore, I love it, and it has stuck with me ever since.

Teach your students the spirit of *Aloha*. When they get to your room, they are starting fresh. When they are leaving, leave it all behind. It seems silly, but it works. It is almost like they know they will be forgiven there, even if they are not anywhere else. The pressure is off. They can be themselves. I have seen some teachers try to force it, which backfires. However, if you just make it something casual, a part of your classroom mantra, if you will, and especially if the students are taught what it means, you will see a difference.

I had a student who chose me for his senior English project, writing a letter to the teacher who had the biggest impact on his high school career. He said that sometimes he struggled with the other kids, but when he got to my room every day, he knew he could relax, be himself, and no one would judge him. Yes, I cried. That is the power of this.

The Problem: The Kids Who Fall Through the Cracks

This one is more of a long-term project, but the outcomes are incredible. Years ago, there was a movement on Education Twitter called "Good Calls Home." The gist is what we have known for years: You should contact home for good, not just the bad. We all know this is harder to manage than it isn't. The good news usually gets away from us.

I liked the concept, but I also felt it perpetually props up the good kids. While credit should always be given where it is due, I started doing something a little differently.

The Action: Send Postcards Home

Here is what I did:

1. I found a nice quote and put four on a page.
2. I copied it on cardstock and cut it up.
3. I bought postcard stamps (much cheaper than regular stamps).
4. Once a week, I picked one kid who would normally either be a big pain or would otherwise fall through the cracks.
5. I watched and waited until they did something noteworthy.
6. On Fridays, I sent home a postcard bragging about that student.

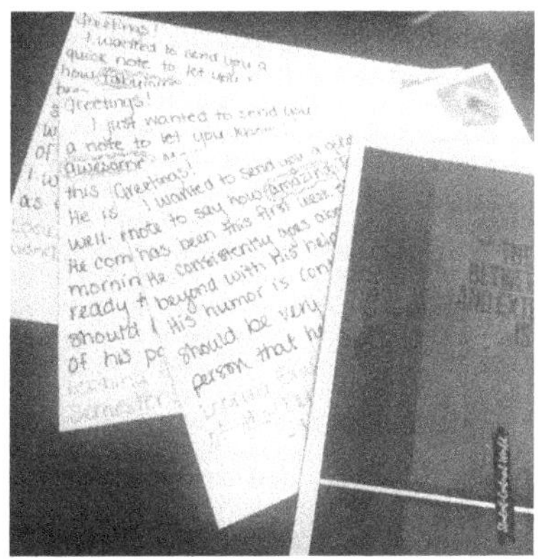

There were many layers to this. First, I never told the students I did this. Even when they would bring it up, I would play dumb and say I had no idea what they were talking about. (But I would always give the recipient a sly wink so they did not think it was fake.) Think of the impact. This kid is usually the one getting the opposite calls home or no acknowledgment at all. I remember the first time I did this. It was right before Back-to-

School Night. The mom came in purely to ask if I got her son mixed up with somebody else.

Here's the best part. When it is a postcard, *everyone* can see it —the good in this child.

The next day, that child acts a little bit better. Tries a little bit harder. I do not know of anyone who has done this and not had that reaction. The key is to expect nothing from this. Just put some good karma out into the world for a student who may not normally get it. Anything else is an added bonus.

The Problem: The Spoon-Fed Generation

We are currently teaching a spoon-fed generation of students who want answers just handed to them. They avoid adversity and do not want to work harder than what comes easily. They have grown up with answers at their fingertips. Need to know the capital of Madagascar? Google it. Forgot how to solve a math problem? Watch a three-minute video tutorial. Want to settle a debate with a friend? Pull out your phone. For these students, information has always been instant, effortless, and free.

The unintended consequence? Many of them have never had to struggle for an answer. They have never had to sit with a problem, try a solution, fail, and try again. When something does not come easily, their instinct is not to persevere. It is to ask for help, look up the answer, or give up entirely. They have been accidentally trained to believe that learning should be fast and frictionless.

This is not laziness. It is conditioning, and it is not their fault. It does mean that when you give them an assignment that requires real thinking, like trial and error, problem-solving, or taking multiple attempts, they may push back. They may say it is too hard. They may wait for you to give them the answer. They may shut down entirely. Not because they are incapable, but because they have never been taught how to work through difficulty.

The Action: Do Not Give Them an Out

Here are three questioning techniques that work like a charm in situations where this happens.

Technique 1: When a student tells you they need help, ask, "What three things have you already tried to find a solution?" This engages their independence and critical thinking.

Technique 2: If they come back with "Nothing," ask, "What is *one* thing you can try?" Do not let them quit. Make them work for it. They will get uncomfortable. That is okay. Change is uncomfortable.

Technique 3: If you get the inevitable "I dunno," jump in and add "...yet." *You do not know yet.* This shows the expectation of a growth mindset and might be the first time they have been pushed with both expectation and security.

Then walk them through the issue to help them get where they need to be. The whole interaction might not be a home run, but it will be a win.

The Problem: Our Own Triggers

As I mentioned before, our kids are not the only ones who need a growth mindset; we do, too. Nowhere is that more obvious than in those moments when a student's behavior sends us over the edge. Something happens in class, and you get angry, upset, or disappointed. Maybe a student rolls their eyes. Maybe they talk back. Maybe they refuse to work. Maybe they just won't stop fidgeting. In that split second, your heart rate spikes, your jaw tightens, and suddenly you are no longer a calm, reflective educator. You are just a frustrated human being trying to survive the next five minutes.

Here is what is really happening: That action triggered you, and there is always a route to why you were triggered. The question is whether you take the time to find it.

Start by asking yourself if this is a student problem or a *you* problem? Are you angry because you would have never been allowed to behave that way in school? That is a you problem. Your own history is not their responsibility. Are you angry because you feel your directions were ignored? Maybe they were being defiant, or maybe your directions were unclear, and they checked out. Only reflection will tell you.

Are you angry because you feel you cannot do your job if they are not doing theirs? That is real. It is also a sign that your classroom systems may not be supporting you the way they should. Are you angry because you had an impression that things should be a certain way, and the student has altered that? That is a you problem. Expectations are not reality. Do you think their behavior is a direct reflection of your worth as a teacher or as a person? If the answer is yes, that is a heavy weight to carry, and it is not true. A student acting out is not a judgment on your value. It is a student acting out.

Some of these are our own issues to work through. Some are frustrations bubbling up from a system that is not supporting our needs. Either way, the first step is recognizing that the trigger exists and naming it.

The Solution: Change Your Response

Once you have identified your trigger, you have a choice. You can keep reacting the same way and getting the same results, or you can change your response. Here is an example. Say you have a student who cannot sit still. He is constantly tapping, shifting, getting up, wandering. It is a huge distraction. It gets under your skin. You have tried consequences with warnings, moving his seat, and sending him out to the hall, but if those consequences were effective, the distractions would no longer be an issue. So why are you still fighting the same battle every day?

Instead of reaching for another punitive consequence, try something different. Ask the student, when he is not distracted, whether he concentrates better when he can move around. Chances are, he will say yes. That is not an excuse. That is data. Then look into options. A makeshift standing desk. Fidget bands on his chair legs. An old-school stress ball he can squeeze under his desk. These are not rewards for bad behavior. They are accommodations for a student whose body is not designed to sit still.

I used to keep a container of stress balls on my desk. The kids who needed them knew they could discreetly take one when they needed to settle. No announcement. No shame. Just a quiet agreement between us. Since it was not out in the open, it never became a toy or a distraction. It just worked.

Remember: A student quietly squeezing a stress ball cannot possibly be more distracting than the behavior you are currently trying to manage.

Also, consider this. Instead of taking away movement from an ornery child, try giving them *more*. I know so many teachers with the mentality: "If they take away my time, I am going to take away theirs," but if that is not purely punitive, I do not know what is... and punitive does not work with this generation. Here is what many teachers do not realize. Our students today get less physical activity than they did years ago. They do not run around outside until dark. They do not climb trees or ride bikes to a friend's house. Physically, many of them lack the core strength to sit still for extended periods. That is not misbehavior. That is biology, and it is true for regular kids, not even those with ADHD or other diagnoses.

The Problem: Not Paying Attention

Let's be honest. Few things are more frustrating than looking out at your class and realizing half of them have checked out. You are explaining something important. You have gone over it twice. And still, a hand goes up, and a student asks, "Wait, what are we supposed to be doing?" It is enough to make you want to pull your hair out.

Here is what we need to understand. The human attention span is roughly seven seconds right now. In 1900, it was around twenty minutes. Things have changed. *Dramatically*. Our students are not choosing to zone out. Their brains are wired differently because of the world they grew up in. Just because we think something is important does not mean they are matching our energy. The problem is not that they are lazy or disrespectful. The problem is that we are expecting them to pay attention in a way their brains no longer know how to. When we get frustrated, when we call them out, when we make them feel bad for zoning out, we are not solving anything. We are just adding shame to the equation.

The Solution: Give Them Grace

This might sound counterintuitive, but we need to give them grace when they zone out. Instead of punishing the behavior, teach them how to handle it. I taught my students, age-appropriately, that if they were going to ask a question or had no idea what was happening, instead of blurting out "What are we doing?" they should preface it by saying:

- "I zoned out for a minute. Can you explain…?" or
- "You might have already said this, but..."

That small shift changed everything. It puts the onus on them for zoning out, but it also acknowledges that sometimes our thoughts can trail off. "I, as your teacher, do not want you to miss things because you did a perfectly natural thing, but own it."

The second part of the solution is about your directions. Write them as if the student were absent and reading without you. Do not assume they were paying attention when you explained it. Do not assume they heard the verbal instructions. Write everything down clearly, step by step. It might take an extra minute or two on the back end, but think how much easier it would be if your instructions were so clear that even someone who was not there would understand. No more repeating yourself. No more confusion. No more "Wait, what are we doing?" and if you're snarky like me, hang a poster that says, "Have you read the directions?" and point to it. It is fun when the kids start doing it too. That's positive peer pressure.

The bottom line? Meet them where they are. Their attention spans are shorter. That is not going to change. How do you respond to it? That is entirely up to you. Remember: Our kids just want love and guidance. Let us give them that.

These five actions are not magic fixes, and they will not transform your classroom overnight. But they are starting points—tangible, doable steps you can take tomorrow. Pick one. Try it. See what happens. You do not need to overhaul everything at once. You just need to interrupt the pattern.

Apathy does not usually arrive all at once, and it does not leave all at once either. It recedes little by little, one student at a time, as you consistently show them that their voice matters, their effort is noticed, and their presence in your room means something. That is the real work, and it starts with a single step.

The beauty of starting small is that it gives you room to breathe. You are not overhauling your entire practice. You are picking one thing, trying it, and watching what changes. Maybe it works right away. Maybe it needs tweaking. Either way, you are gathering information and showing your students that something is different. They may not say it out loud, but they notice when the adult in the room is making an effort. That alone can begin to shift the culture.

Here is something else to keep in mind: you will not reach every student at the same time. Don't let that discourage you.

Apathy is often a shell built up over years of feeling unseen or unheard. That shell does not crack all at once. But when you keep showing up, when you keep making it clear that their effort matters and their voice counts, the shell starts to weaken. One student engages. Then another. Before you know it, the room feels different. Not because you flipped a switch, but because you kept taking small, steady steps in the right direction.

Reflection Questions for this chapter...

I emphasize a "gradual release of responsibility." On a scale of 1 to 10, how hands-off are you right now? **What would it look like to dial it back a notch?**

The Help Wanted board allowed students to help each other without copying answers. **How could you create a similar system?** What would need to be in place for it to work?

The Mastery Schedule gives students windows of time rather than strict daily deadlines. **How might this change the dynamic in your classroom?** What concerns would you need to address?

The chapter ends with a reminder about growth mindset for teachers. Think of a recent lesson that did not go as planned. **What did you learn from it?** What will you tweak next time?

Try This Tomorrow:

Choose one of these organizational strategies to try:

Strategy	Try This
Share the unit schedule	*On the first day of your next unit, give students a one-page schedule with topics, essential questions, and the test date.*
Create a daily plan board	*Post each day's tasks, required work, and optional early finisher activities where all students can see them.*
Try a Help Wanted board	*Use sticky notes or magnets. Have students signal when they are available to help peers with quick questions.*
Give a mastery schedule	*For a short unit (1–2 weeks), list assignments and the window of time students have to complete each one. Let them choose the order.*

After trying one of these, jot down one observation. What surprised you? What would you adjust?

CHAPTER 9
EFFECTIVE CLASSROOM DISCIPLINE

You can always identify a school with a crumbling discipline culture, and it's not because referrals pile up, but because teachers stopped writing them altogether. Why? Because nothing ever comes of them other than a student being sent back to class with a smile and a smirk. So, what do these teachers do? They quietly adapt, lowering expectations and closing their doors just to survive the day. From the outside, it looks peaceful. Inside, it is survival mode with no end in sight. When consequences vanish, so does accountability. Everyone just goes through the motions.

This is especially tough because you may have an idea of your perfect utopian classroom that you subconsciously strive for. The children sit there, excited to learn every day. They hang on your every word. They do exactly what you want. But we know that does not seem to happen anymore. In fact, it seems like it is happening less and less.

The behavior issues that did not even occur a couple of years ago are now commonplace across the board. The kids who used to be considered "good kids" are now causing issues, making comments, and becoming distractions. Other kids are shutting down. They cannot concentrate. They cannot get their work done. They do not want to be part of the riffraff, yet somehow they are all getting dragged into it. You have tried punishment, taking things away, and calling home. It seems like none of it is working.

You are not alone. A lot of the discipline strategies we use in the classroom are outdated or not quite right for the generation of kids we have in front of us. That does not mean there should be no consequences for improper behavior, but it does mean that *how* we structure those consequences should look different. So why is this happening? Is it us? Generally speaking, it is not your classroom management that sets off these issues. It is actually the factors we cannot control that are contributing to these behaviors. Many of them relate to Adverse Childhood Experiences (ACEs).

The CDC has identified a list of adverse childhood experiences that contribute to trauma: physical abuse, emotional abuse, sexual abuse, physical neglect, emotional neglect, a mother treated violently, household substance abuse, household mental illness, parental separation or divorce, and an incarcerated household member. Some seem rare, but we know from our training that they are not as rare as we think. Let us be honest, many of us have probably gone through at least one of these ourselves.

We never know how many students come into our classrooms who may not have support at home and who may be dealing with trauma. Looking at the impact of childhood trauma, we see effects on brain development, cognition, physical health, emotions, relationships, mental health, and behavior. When students are in these situations, their hierarchy of needs is not being met at home. I am not saying it is our job to fix it—we cannot—but we need to understand that if basic needs are not met, higher learning cannot happen. They cannot learn appropriately. They cannot behave appropriately. These students may be looking for attention, guidance, or lashing out. Behavior is always the symptom, not the source. There is a need for that child that is not being met. We still need to find a way to make it all work.

Understanding vs. Accepting Behavior

There is a fine line between understanding behavior and accepting behavior. Understanding why a student is in a crisis moment—why they lashed out, shut down, or refused to work—does not mean excusing what they did. It means recognizing that the behavior is a symptom, not the root cause. The root cause might be trauma, hunger, exhaustion, fear, or any number of things you cannot see from your desk. But the behavior still happened. The assignment still has not been done. The other students still witnessed the disruption. Accountability cannot simply disappear. It has to look different.

Here is what accountability looks like when you truly understand behavior. Instead of asking, "What is wrong with you?" you ask, "What happened?" Instead of a detention that isolates and punishes, you have a restorative conversation that repairs and teaches. Instead of assuming the student knows how to regulate their emotions, assume they do not and show them how. Accountability becomes less about consequences and more about conversations. Less about punishment and more about practice. The goal is not to make the student suffer for what they did. The goal is to help them learn a better way so they do not do it again.

This is not soft. It is not permissive. It is actually harder than handing out a detention. It takes time. It takes patience. It takes a willingness to sit in discomfort with a student who may not have anyone else sitting with them. But it is the only approach that actually changes behavior long-term, because a student who is only punished learns to hide better. A student who is understood learns to try again. That is the difference between managing a classroom and leading one.

Check Your Own Triggers

I know I mentioned this earlier, but it deserves a revisit right now. Is there an issue, or are you just triggered? When you are frustrated, why are you being triggered? Is it an unrealistic expectation? Think about their age. How long have they been sitting still? What are you asking of them?

Are you triggered by disrespect? If so, why? Is it because you feel you are an authority figure who should be respected at all costs? Is it because the disruption is affecting everyone? Is it that the child is disrespecting themselves, and that upsets you?

A dysregulated adult can never regulate a dysregulated child. When you are at your boiling point—and we have all been there—you cannot get a kid to do the right thing when you are frustrated, angry, or yelling. You cannot force respect. Respect develops. It is sometimes earned. It needs to be learned, but not in a way you can force.

Take a moment. Give the kids a two-minute brain break so you can also have one. Have a coworker watch the class so you can run to the bathroom or refill your water bottle. Regulate yourself so you can help regulate the child. The more you can do proactively, the less you will have to do reactively.

We have all been in a situation where two students are not getting along, and you say, "I cannot make that person like you, but we can at least get along." The same principle applies here. Find the balance. Model the respect you want to see. Take time to emphasize students who are behaving properly, and when the misbehaving student does something right, find a way to point it out. Sometimes they do not know what to do with positive interactions. They may balk. They may even behave worse. Tread lightly. Slip a piece of candy on their desk. Leave them a note.

Acknowledge them to the whole class if that is what they need. It is a kid-by-kid process.

Problem-Solving Over Punishment

Ultimately, we need to revamp how we think about discipline. Instead of defaulting to punishment, we need to focus on problem-solving. Here is an example:

Say you have a student who is consistently late. The policy says they receive a detention. That detention might feel like a deterrent, but if it does not actually change the behavior, it is useless. The consequence is not having the intended effect. So instead of doubling down on punishment, try problem-solving. Figure out *why* the student is late. Is it a transportation issue? Are they coming from a class on the other side of the building? Is something happening at home in the mornings? Once you know the root cause, you can actually address it. Punishment alone will not fix what you do not understand.

This is where understanding the different types of consequences and reinforcements helps.

Reinforcement is about increasing desired behaviors. *Positive reinforcement* means adding something good to encourage a behavior. Giving a student a sticker for turning in homework on time is positive reinforcement. *Negative reinforcement* means removing something unpleasant to encourage a behavior. If you stop reminding a student to stay on task once they start working, that is negative reinforcement—you are taking away the nagging because they are doing what they are supposed to do.

Punishment is about decreasing unwanted behaviors. *Positive punishment* means adding something unpleasant to decrease a behavior. Giving a student extra homework for talking out of turn is positive punishment. *Negative punishment* means removing something pleasant to decrease a behavior. Taking away recess because a student was disruptive is negative punishment. The challenge is that punishment often stops the behavior in the moment, but does not teach the student what *to* do instead.

Consequences are cause-and-effect reactions. *Natural consequences* happen without any adult intervention. If a student refuses to wear a coat, they get cold. If they do not turn in an assignment, they get a zero. Natural consequences are wonderful —a lot of us call this karma. However, waiting for a natural consequence might be too dangerous. "Do not run in the street because you might get hit by a car" is not a natural consequence we want to see. *Logical consequences* are directly related to the behavior. If a student makes a mess, they clean it up. If they are late to class, they owe that time back. In most school situations, logical consequences are the most useful. *Unnatural consequences* have no logical connection to the behavior. Taking away computer time because a student was throwing paper is unnatural—one has nothing to do with the other. Natural and logical consequences tend to be more effective because they teach cause and effect. Unnatural consequences often feel arbitrary and can breed resentment instead of accountability.

As teachers, we most often use unnatural consequences and negative punishment. These seem like they should be a last resort. Are they necessary at times? Absolutely. Sometimes nothing else works. But why do we use them right away? Plainly stated, they are the easiest to make a blanket policy with. "If you do this, this is going to happen." We think that if we tell students ahead of time, they will not do it. However, this does not work like it used to. Often, when these are implemented with a student who has trauma, it will intensify their reactions because they do not know how to regulate their emotions or behavior.

I once saw a question. "What do teachers and administrators believe motivates people but does not?" Answers included blanket policies, dress-down days, little trinkets, fear, guilt, and asking for input and ignoring it. We get frustrated as adults when these things happen to us, but do we not also do this in the classroom? One of my favorite sayings about parenting is "We are not raising children. We are raising adults." Why would it be acceptable for us to get frustrated that these motivational tactics are a waste when these are the same tactics we are trying to use with our children?

Resentment vs. Accountability

Much of this comes down to resentment versus accountability. When a consequence is delivered, is it causing resentment or accountability? Are students learning why what they did was incorrect and what they can do in the future? Or is it just something dished out because someone is frustrated? It is hard. One reason we go to blanket policies is because it is difficult to take care of one or two students while still caring for everyone else. That is why having a plan is so important.

It is important to de-escalate and then have a restorative conversation. It is not just about the punishment. It is "Listen, X happened; therefore, Y happened. Let us talk about it. Let us figure this out. If this happens again, then what? What should we do?"

Ask the student the next steps. They are not going to say, "I think I should lose recess." Maybe they will come up with something that actually works for them. Maybe it is the first time anyone has given them that autonomy. "Do this because I said so" creates resentment instead of accountability.

In 9 out of 10 cases of behavioral issues, the student is not giving you a hard time. *They* are having a hard time. We are just the ones responsible for dealing with it. If an incident is happening, step back and think about what happened right before. Kids can get triggered for reasons we do not know. If we go right to punishing, it can backfire. Jot down what happened before a behavior. You might catch trends you had not noticed. We cannot change a student's behavior, but we can change how we respond to it. They need to be held accountable for their behavior; it is just a matter of how.

There is data that sociopaths and psychopaths can show tendencies as young as age four. The No. 1 commonality is that they are not held accountable for their actions. If nothing else, it is important to do those small bits we can. As the adult in the room, it is a mindset shift. We need to prevent the behavior from happening again.

Will kids still act up? Yes. Will you still have *that kid*? Yes, but if you create a culture that helps everyone regulate themselves, resolve conflicts, understand expectations, and know the routines, the whole process becomes much easier.

The Punishment Must Fit the Crime

The main thing to remember is that the consequence needs to fit the action. Whatever you implement needs to fit what is happening to actually have a result. You might try many things, and it seems like nothing is working, but if you see little inklings of a chance, that is the road to run down. If something bigger is happening and they are not responding to your discipline, they are not going to in the future. Decide if you will keep fighting, keep trying, or refer it because it is beyond your pay grade.

Children need to learn the rules. But consider this distinction: If you say, "The expectation is X, Y, Z," they cannot break an expectation, but they can break a rule. It is a semantics game that makes a difference. You may be the only person who emphasizes being courteous, kind, and considerate. If you can work that into your behavior management plan, you will see it returned tenfold.

You also want to be mindful of what you choose as a consequence. Some states are trying to make it illegal for teachers to cancel recess as a punishment. Many teachers are outraged. I watched a thread of people saying, "We cannot even give kids consequences anymore." There are reasons why taking away recess is a bad idea. If you take away the one chance students can release energy, especially if you are not adding brain breaks, movement, flexible seating, and ways to fidget, you will have the same problems. The student cannot get their energy out. Human beings are not meant to sit still or be quiet for long periods. They need breaks, mentally and physically. As I mentioned before, students today are fidgety because it is not like it was back in the day. They would get home from school, go outside, and play for hours. Their bodies were getting a workout. That does not happen as much anymore. Their bodies physically cannot sit still because they are not getting the correct amount of movement.

Beyond that, it is so important to remember that no kid wants to be bad. No kid wants to feel bad about themselves. So often, it is a defense mechanism. If a kid is giving you a hard time, they are having a hard time. You, as the grown-up, need to help them learn to regulate.

Trauma recovery has three levels, like an avocado. The outer peel is what people see: how they act—good, bad, or indifferent. The middle part is the feelings, mental health symptoms, and triggers. That makes up the largest part. The pit is the memories, beliefs about themselves or the world based on that trauma, or the shame. What we see is the outer peel. The pit is the hardest to break through. The feelings part is all over the place. If we want to regulate behaviors, we need to help the student regulate that "squishy middle," so the outer peel stays fresh for everyone else. Can we fix the pit? No. That is not our job, but we can help a student learn to regulate the middle and pass the information along to the powers that be to help them get to the pit.

Developing Your Behavior Plan

Now, let us come up with a plan. Think about the biggest discipline issues you currently have. Write them down. There might be two or twenty-two. Look at all of them and figure out which is the worst problem. Is it one particular student? Or is something going on overall that is taking away from your ability to teach?

Let me go through an example with you, a silly one that happened in my classroom. I had a group that was continually throwing paper. It was a disturbance. It was a mess. Kids were running out of supplies. So for mine, the problem was throwing paper.

Type	Example for Throwing Paper
Positive Reinforcement	*Groups receive points each day if they are not throwing paper*
Negative Reinforcement	*Calling home*
Positive Punishment	*Receiving detention*
Negative Punishment	*Losing inquiry time*
Natural Consequence	*They do not get more supplies*
Logical Consequence	*They stay after class and clean up*
Unnatural Consequence	*Writing an essay on proper classroom behavior*

It is important to determine how you want to proceed with these in an attempt to deter the behavior. Here is the order I came up with:

1. **Logical consequence:** Stay after class and clean up. This makes the most sense. It is not a knee-jerk reaction. It is, "You did this; therefore, this follows."
2. **Positive reinforcement:** Groups earn points if they do not throw paper. Reward the kids who are not acting like fools. This adds positive peer pressure.
3. **Natural consequence:** They do not get more supplies. (This also adds peer pressure.)
4. **Positive punishment:** Detention or coming during lunch.
5. **Negative punishment:** Lose inquiry time. (This is like recess. Losing a love of learning is a last option.)
6. **Negative reinforcement:** Calling home. Keep this until last.

You always want to document this as well. This way, when it comes down to it, you will have data to back it up. Say a parent or administrator questions what is going on. You can easily pull out your data and say, "On this day, he had to stay after class and clean up. On this day, she made her group lose points. On this day, they needed supplies and could not get them." When you call home or go to an administrator, you can say, "Here is the list of everything I have tried. Here is when it happened. Here was the response. What would you suggest?" It is twofold: You are changing behaviors and covering yourself.

A Note on Violence Against Teachers

We are having more instances of violence against teachers. Unfortunately, teachers are not always supported. Hopefully, this is not an issue you have encountered, but I want to touch on a few points that everyone should know.

Full disclaimer: This is a suggested list. Always defer to your union and school rules.

- File a police report. If a student attacks you and you are not getting support, file a report. This starts a paper trail.
- Demand that your school pay for training. Learn how to defend yourself or, if necessary, physically restrain a student.
- Contact OSHA about unsafe working conditions.
- Contact the EEOC. They could possibly help.
- Know your state laws about teacher rights.
- Look into Workers' Compensation. If you get hurt and are not supported, go to the doctor and document everything.

Hopefully, none of you have to deal with this, but I would be remiss not to put it out there.

A New Way Forward

None of this is meant to overwhelm you. If anything, it is meant to lift the weight off your shoulders. You are not a bad teacher because you are struggling with behaviors that did not exist a few years ago. You are not failing because the old strategies are not landing the way they used to. The game changed, and no one gave you a new playbook. What matters is that you are still in the room. You are still showing up and looking for answers, which means you have not given up on your students, even on the hard days.

The data and strategies we just walked through are not about creating some magical, utopian classroom where nothing ever goes wrong. That classroom does not exist. What they are about is giving you tools that actually match the kids sitting in front of you right now. Tools that restore accountability without relying on systems that no longer work. Tools that help you stop surviving and start breathing again. You did not become a teacher to close your door and count down the minutes. You became a teacher to make a difference, and you still can. It just requires a different approach that is built for this generation, in this moment, with all the messiness that comes with it.

Reflection Questions for this chapter...

Think about a recent behavior issue. Did you respond with punishment or problem-solving? What was the outcome?

What is one small change you could make to be more proactive (rather than reactive) with discipline?

The chapter distinguishes between natural, logical, and unnatural consequences. Which type do you use most often? Which would be most effective for your current biggest behavior challenge?

"In nine out of ten cases, the student is not giving you a hard time. They are having a hard time." Think of a student who challenges you. What "hard time" might they be having that you cannot see?

Try This Tomorrow:

Choose one of these strategies to try this week:

Strategy	Try This
Identify your triggers	*The next time a student frustrates you, ask, "Is this a student problem or a me problem?" Write down your answer.*
Logical consequence	*Instead of a blanket punishment, ask, "What consequence directly connects to this action?" Implement that.*
Data tracking	*For one behavior issue this week, jot down what happened right before the behavior. Look for patterns.*
Restorative conversation	*After a behavior incident, sit down with the student and ask, "What happened? What should we do next time? What do you need from me?"*
Positive reinforcement	*Catch one student doing something right. Point it out publicly (or privately, if that works better).*

After trying one of these, jot down one observation. What surprised you? What would you adjust?

CHAPTER 10
BUILDING MEANINGFUL RELATIONSHIPS

Getting to know your students on a personal level is the bread and butter of everything we are discussing. The more you know about your students, the more you can adjust your classroom environment to support how they learn best and how you can best hook them. However, as we all know in education, being asked, "Have you tried building a relationship with them?" has become the proverbial nails on a chalkboard when it comes from an administrator. *Are they for real?*

The issue is not the question itself. It is the nuance behind it. It has become a generalized question, almost a dig, really, without any guiding substance to back it up. We all know we want good relationships with our students, but so many of us were never trained to understand how engagement, relationships, and activity completion work together. Getting to know your students and their intent is everything when it comes to crafting a lesson and ensuring it goes smoothly, yet the expectation is that we already know how to do this. Most of us were trained in everything *but* actual classroom management, and when we were, it was not realistic. Our first experiences in the actual classroom were more trial by fire than anything else.

To understand student intent, you need to understand what

makes your students tick. What gets them excited? What matters to them outside your classroom? This comes down to rapport and relationships, the intentional work of knowing more about your students as the school year progresses. It can start with something as simple as knowing their favorite song or movie and grow into an understanding of their hopes and dreams. From there, you need to figure out how to weave that information into your everyday lessons, seamlessly connecting their world to your content.

Most teachers see this as a giant undertaking. Impractical. A waste of time. Honestly, given how little time we have and how many students we have, it is easy to see why they feel that way. They think it is not possible with their subject matter or their age group. But here is what they miss: This basic concept hooks students faster than anything else. Ignoring it is a real waste of time. Plus, I've said it before, and I'll say it again, this doesn't actually take more time on your end. You're just repackaging what you already do to have a different outcome.

This all comes down to understanding the generation currently in our classrooms.

Many people feel that our current students are laid back, that you cannot engage them, and that they have no interest in being there. But if they *buy into* a topic, if they really get excited, the sky is the limit. This is because of how they are wired. They have grown up in a society with different factors in play than previous generations, and we have to meet them where they are, not where we were.

The Atmosphere of Your Classroom

As woo-woo as it sounds, everything starts with the vibe of your classroom atmosphere. When I say atmosphere, I don't just mean where you put your desks. I mean the actual *feel* and *climate* of your entire classroom. Think of a moment when you felt *out of place*. You did not feel right. You were a little on edge. Maybe you couldn't figure out why you were, but you felt uncomfortable. Our students feel this in our classrooms more often than you would imagine. If you want students of this generation to buy in, they have to feel comfortable doing so.

For instance, I had a sign in my classroom with FAIL in large letters, and it said: FIRST ATTEMPT IN LEARNING. Mind-blowing for them. Without fail, one of them would always bring it up in every class period within the first week of school. It sparked some great conversations that helped build a sense of class unity. They knew from my pushing these ideas that we were going to try hard, find ways to work together, and piece it all together. I constantly heard about the atmosphere from my kids: how I ran the class, my teaching style, everything. It was so different, and they loved it… and they felt comfortable saying so.

It's all about opening the lines of communication where a student isn't afraid to ask questions or speak their mind (you may need to model how to do this respectfully now and again; they are still children, mind you). However, classroom communication is everything. Most of the time, when there is an issue with a student, parent, or administrator, a communication breakdown is the reason. Someone misunderstood or was unclear. When you have the systems and processes in place like we've been talking about, this happens much less. The flow works much better.

I am not saying you will never have an issue, but when you make communication changes part of the culture, the volume of issues will decrease exponentially.

Recognizing the Little Things

All of this ties into understanding Social-Emotional Learning (SEL). SEL got a terrible rollout. Many teachers heard the concept, their school started pushing it, and there was a deep sigh and eye roll. "What is this? Something else on our plate?" Right now, SEL is more important than ever. We are in a difficult time after coming off a difficult time. Our students are young and trying to process changes. SEL should not be extra work. It should not be a set curriculum. (Some schools tried to make it a curriculum that teachers had to add on. That is not it.) SEL is implemented in the day-to-day. Little things here and there.

The kids need to be able to express emotions. Our current generations are not as socially adept at this as previous generations. We can blame the internet, social media, whatever, but the bottom line is, we see our kids so much during the day. If we can incorporate understanding feelings and what to *do* with them without extra work, just implementing it here and there, a quick side note, not taking extra time, and incorporating it into what we already do, the results are incredible. We will help these kids for the rest of their lives, not just while they are in our class.

One way to do this is through classroom recognition, even in small ways. Most teachers award students in some way. Younger grades have prize boxes. Older grades give extra credit. Schoolwide, we recognize high grades, perfect attendance, and impeccable behavior. While those have merit, are they what we should focus on day to day? Are we awarding the best things that make a long-term difference?

Should we still recognize those things? Yes, but we need to spend time recognizing the little things, the things that build character. Some students struggle academically. Some have illnesses or issues at home. Some have undiagnosed learning disabilities or other reasons their behavior is not on point. If you recognize the little things, like character-based traits or innate moments that show who a student really is, they have a more lasting effect than the obvious kids who do well. If a student feels valued and has achieved something, you will have a better relationship with that student and with the others because they recognize what you see. The climate, engagement, and relationships will be amazing.

We can bring this same mindset to content assignments, too. Let me be clear: I am not saying we should stop holding students accountable for their work, but we need to move past the old way of thinking... the "If it is this late, you lose this many points" approach. That system does not actually teach responsibility. It just punishes late work without addressing why it was late in the first place, which throws the relationship piece right out the window.

Here is what I have found works most consistently. As I mentioned, I assigned activities that students genuinely needed to complete to move forward, not just assignments to fill the grade book. Then I put a simple system in place for late work and absences. If a student did not turn something in, they had to fill out a form explaining why. Nothing complicated. Just a date, their name, the assignment, and a short explanation (some years I used checkboxes with an "Other" section where they could write more). It was always handwritten and always required their signature. That form did two things. First, it made the student pause and reflect on why the work was missing. Second, it created a paper trail. When a student repeatedly failed to turn in work, I had documentation to guide a conversation with them, their parents, or an administrator.

I also kept a filing cabinet in my room with files marked by class period and day of the week. Any work we did that day went into that folder. If a student was absent, it was their responsibility to check the folder. They could also refer to our unit schedule and due-date calendar to make sure they had everything. This put the ownership on them, but also made it easy for them to take responsibility.

I saw the difference immediately. Students stopped saying "I did not know it was due," because the form forced them to acknowledge the missed deadline. I had a student once get angry about a zero. "But I wasn't here, so how could I have done it?" Before I could even respond, another student at my desk started rattling off the make-up procedures. That is when I knew my system was working. The students knew the expectations because the system was consistent, fair, and focused on accountability rather than punishment.

I stopped focusing on points and started focusing on mastery, and the students found a groove that followed. Yes, you may have to remind them where the filing cabinet is, especially if they have not been absent before, but once they understand the procedure, they know what to do. You can always make an anchor chart to hang up that reminds them of the steps when they come back after an absence. There is a better way than "If it is late, you lose points." For every moment when a student turns something in, or doesn't, there is a better system… and it works.

The Power of Brain Breaks

When we hear "brain breaks," many of us picture little kids with endless energy who need to be calmed down, but that is not necessarily what brain breaks are or who they are for. The truth is, it is impossible for any human being to be on our game 100 percent of the time. Adults, teenagers, and young children all hit mental walls. The difference is that adults have learned (often unconsciously) how to step away and reset. We get a glass of water. We take a quick walk around the office. We scroll our phones for sixty seconds. Those are brain breaks. We just don't call them that.

Our students have not learned this skill, or at least how to do it appropriately. They don't know how to recognize when their focus is slipping or what to do about it. That is where we come in. Brain breaks are short, intentional pauses in instruction that give students time to decompress so they can return to learning at their full potential. They do not take much time, often just one or two minutes, but they make a massive difference in student engagement, behavior, and overall classroom climate.

Remember, research shows that frequent brain breaks are necessary, especially for younger children, because many students today lack the core strength of previous generations.

With less recess, fewer students walking to school, and less unstructured outdoor play, their bodies are not built to sit still for extended periods. Expecting them to do so is not just unrealistic; it is setting everyone up for frustration. Brain breaks are not a reward or a distraction. They are a physiological necessity for learning to happen.

Types of Brain Breaks

There are many different kinds of brain breaks, and the right choice depends on what your students need in that moment. Some breaks are energizing, designed to wake up a sleepy class or shift sluggish energy. Think quick movement activities like a thirty-second dance party or even just having everyone stand up and stretch. Other breaks are calming, meant to bring down a class that is overly hyper, anxious, or dysregulated. These might include deep breathing exercises, a quiet two-minute drawing prompt, or listening to a calming song with eyes closed.

The key is matching the break to the moment. An energized class needs a calming break. A lethargic class needs an energizing break. A class that is simply "off" might just need a reset, something neutral like everyone standing up, touching their nose, and sitting back down. The break itself does not have to be complicated. It just has to be a deliberate pause.

Brain breaks can be done with the whole class, in small groups, or even individually. Some teachers build them into transitions between subjects. Others use them when they notice attention lagging. You can also create a "brain break station" in your classroom where students can quietly take a moment on their own when they need to reset, no questions asked. I used to have a bulletin board with a blank adult coloring book spread across it, along with a container of markers. My students used to police themselves, go color for a few minutes, and sit back down. No one, and I mean no one, thought that it was going to work without pandemonium breaking out. However, I tried it, and not only did it work beautifully, but other colleagues quickly followed suit.

How to Implement Brain Breaks Naturally

The best brain breaks are the ones that don't feel like another thing to plan. You don't need a separate lesson or a complicated setup. Start small. Pick one transition time, maybe between reading and math, and add a two-minute brain break there. See what happens. If your class is dragging after lunch, try a quick energizer before diving into new content. If they come back from recess wound up, try a calming reset. My seventh-grade English teacher used to have us stand up and play Simon Says for a few minutes. As a 12-year-old, I thought she was just quirky, but now I get it.

You can also use brain breaks proactively. Build them into your schedule at regular intervals, just like you would a bathroom break or a transition. Every 20 to 30 minutes of instruction, take 60 seconds to reset. This is not lost time. It is an investment in the time that follows. Students will return to their work more focused, more regulated, and more ready to learn. Here is the best part: Brain breaks work for you, too. When you give the class a two-minute break, you also get a two-minute break. You can reset your own energy, take a sip of water, or just breathe. A regulated adult is the most powerful tool in any classroom. Brain breaks help everyone get there together.

For more ideas, I have broken down dozens of brain breaks by age level and purpose on my website.[1]

All in all, "building meaningful relationships" is not a separate task to add to your overflowing plate. It is the *foundation* upon which everything else is built. When students feel known,

---

1. You can find the full series at studentcenteredworld.com/brain-breaks. From energizing activities for high schoolers to calming resets for elementary students, there is something for every classroom.

they engage differently. When they feel safe, they take risks. When they feel valued, they try harder. When they feel connected, they behave better. None of this requires giant gestures or hours of extra work. It requires intention. Noticing the little things. Showing up consistently. Remembering that the kid giving you a hard time is likely having a hard time. You have the power to be the one person who makes a student feel like they belong. That is not a small thing. That is everything.

The truth is, you probably already know which students need more of this from you. Their names come to mind without much effort. You know the ones who walk in with their guard up, the ones who push you away because they have learned that adults do not stick around. You do not need a new program or a school-wide initiative to reach them. You just need to decide that they are worth the effort, even when they do not make it easy. A quick conversation in the hallway. A genuine, "I noticed you were not yourself today. Is everything okay?" A simple, "I am glad you are here." Those small moments add up in ways you may never see but can trust are happening.

Don't underestimate what this does for you, too. Teaching is harder when you are constantly at odds with your students. It drains you. But when you start building those connections, something shifts. The kid who used to derail your lesson becomes the kid who reminds the class to settle down. The student who never turned anything in starts handing in work because they do not want to disappoint you. That shift does not happen because you cracked down harder. It happens because you built a bridge. Suddenly, you are not spending all your energy managing behavior. You are spending it teaching. That is a better way to work. That is a classroom you actually want to walk into.

The ripple effect goes beyond just those one or two students. When you build genuine connections with the kids who are hardest to reach, the rest of the class notices. They see you treating that student with patience and dignity, even when they do not deserve it by any conventional measure. That does something to the culture of your room. It sends a message louder than any poster on your wall ever could: in here, you are safe. In here, you will be given a fair shot. In here, you are more than the worst thing you have ever done. That kind of culture does not happen by accident. It happens because you decided to be intentional about relationships, even when it was inconvenient, even when it was hard, even when it felt like you were getting nothing in return. Keep showing up. The return is coming, often when you least expect it.

Reflection Questions for this chapter...

What is one small, low-effort way you could learn something new about one student this week?

On a scale of 1 to 10, how safe do your students feel taking risks or making mistakes?

What is one thing you could change to move that number up?

What is one two-minute brain break you could use tomorrow to reset your class when energy is low, or chaos is high?

SEL is described as "little tiny things here and there." What is one tiny thing you could add this week to help students name or manage their emotions?

Try This Tomorrow:

Choose one of these relationship-building strategies to try this week:

Strategy	Try This
The "FAIL" sign	*Put up a sign (even on scratch paper) that says "FAIL = First Attempt In Learning." Point to it when a student is frustrated with a mistake.*
Recognize a "little thing"	*Notice one small act of kindness, effort, or character today. Acknowledge it publicly or with a quick private word.*
SEL check-in	*Ask, "On a scale of 1 to 5, how are you feeling right now?" No explanation needed. Just let them name it.*
Two-minute brain break	*Try "Stand up. Touch your nose. Touch your elbow. Touch your knee. Sit down." That is it. Resets the room.*

After trying one of these, jot down one observation. What changed in your classroom or in your own mindset?

CHAPTER 11
BEATING TEACHER BURNOUT

Before we even get started, I want to tell you that I am proud of you.

That might sound weird. Why would I start a chapter by saying that? It is simple. I am proud of you for taking the initiative to find a way to get back to being you. You would not be reading this if you did not find yourself in a place that seems far from where you came from. A place that has you questioning how you even got here. That question is easier to answer than you think. Why? Because in your soul, you are a good teacher.

Read that again. You are a good teacher.

As educators, we pour so much of ourselves into others that our cups often run dry. At that point, we should recognize the moment and use self-care strategies to regroup and refill, but all too often, we do not. There is no one reason why. Pride. Being trained to believe everyone else's needs come before our own. Feeling it is a sign of weakness. Not knowing how. This is where some become jaded and start counting down to summer. Noses go to the grindstone. We blindly go through the motions. We know we are doing this, but that knowledge makes it worse. Guilt builds. Sometimes we shut down completely.

Maybe next year will be different.

We need to stop that cycle now. It is not fair to our students. Most importantly, it is not fair to us. Teaching is documented as one of the most stressful careers, and it seems like each year we are expected to do more with less. This could be budgetary or school support. It could be the revelation that not all students come to school ready to learn. We know how much distractions or disruptive students can drain a teacher's emotional energy, and we have more students entering our classrooms carrying more emotional baggage than any child should have to carry. How can we expect a student to care about the curriculum if their life outside our walls is in disarray?

So, we try to help them. We give them a safe place. We meet with guidance counselors and parents. We put our souls into saving that one child.

Or we give up and take it personally.

It is almost never personal.

You Cannot Save Everyone

We all have rough days. Our students, even those without trauma, will have off days. Human beings aren't perfect. We cannot expect our students to be perfect, and we cannot expect ourselves to be perfect. If you are doing your best, keeping the class engaged, and your classroom management is on point, then having an off day, or week, or even a school year does not define you as a teacher.

You cannot save everyone.

I have tried. My husband has reminded me many times that I cannot save everyone. He's right, no matter how much we want to resist the idea. The problem is not understanding that. The problem is when it tears us up inside. The thought that there is one student who is not on the path and that there is nothing else we can do to change their trajectory can be debilitating. Sometimes the odds are against us. That does not define you. One day, that student will remember how hard you worked for them.

While you pull for your students, you are also pulling for yourself. We know how much goes into teaching. Lesson planning, content creation, assessment, grading—rinse and repeat. Then factor in IEPs, 504s, meetings, fire drills, and standardized testing. Classes are getting bigger. Bigger classes are harder to control. Losing control stops teaching. With less teaching time, students make less progress. There is a reason "teacher tired" was born. It is okay to be teacher tired. It is okay to have days when you count down to sweatpants and your couch. It is okay to have a rough day. It is okay to take a mental health day.

Stop feeling guilty. Teaching is hard.

Stress vs. Burnout

Teacher stress is real, but on a normal day, it's manageable. What happens when stress becomes too much?

Burnout is different. In helping professions like teaching, burnout results from excessive stress and impossibly high ideals. It leaves people completely drained, disconnected, and unable to function as they used to… and no one is immune. As far back as 2012, teacher burnout crept into the forefront. *HuffPost* referenced a 2012 Gallup report noting that nearly 70 percent of K-12 teachers did not feel fully engaged in their work (Klein, 2014).

Seventy percent. Imagine what it is now.

If you are reading this, you probably recognize the signs of burnout in yourself, yet your passion for education remains. Otherwise, you would not be trying to fix it. You are still a good teacher. You are still the person you were when you set out on this career path. You are just in a difficult season.

Seasons change.

The Three M's to Beating Teacher Burnout

There are what I call the three M's: Mission, Mindset, and Method.

M #1: *Mission*

Mission means *why* you are a teacher. Everyone has a different path. But if you are anything like me, you have always wanted to help others, and teaching became your calling. I live for aha moments. You have moments that make you smile and realize this is why you became a teacher.

But what if those moments are fleeting? Are you truly having fewer warm-and-fuzzy moments, or are they being clouded by other things? Like it or not, you are in charge of your classroom's vibe. Part of your mission is to know what that vibe is like for you, your students, and anyone who walks through the door. You need to define your Mission.

Write down why you wanted to get into education. What drove you? Why did you wake up and say, "I want to teach children"? If your reasoning is about impacting the future generation, you are in the right place. If you were pressured into it, you may have soul-searching to do.

Write down three things you wish to accomplish as a teacher. Not what you want students to do, but three things you wish to hang your hat on. For me, my number one accomplishment was making my classroom feel like the "laid back" one where my students could breathe and let go of the weight of the world. With that, create a mission statement. It does not have to be perfect. It will help you focus each day and fade out the noise.

This mission statement can be fluid. Over the years, mine changed. I began to be drawn to presenting professional development. I was impacting students outside my own classroom. Put your mission statement somewhere you can see it. I hide things under my desk blotter or inside my planner cover so I can look at them whenever I need to, without being obvious.

M #2: *Mindset*

Mindset is everything. Have you ever been in a funk? Murphy's Law kicks in. You start pinpointing every little thing going wrong, even if they are not major. If you were not in a funk, you might not even have noticed them. We have all been there.

Move that into the classroom. A difficult student. An administrator who forgets what it is like to be in the classroom. A helicopter parent. So many factors are outside our control, but we internalize them and try to change ourselves. When that does not work, we doubt our abilities.

That is where you stop. Shift your mindset. Instead of focusing on external factors, focus on what *you* are doing that may affect them. Not every day will be perfect. Lessons will flop. That is okay. Grow from those days instead of branding them as reasons you are doing it wrong. Too many of us pour from an empty cup. It became expected that as a teacher, you are "on" for everyone else all the time. But what about you?

My husband used to get on my case about doing something for myself every once in a while. I always rolled my eyes. How could I be a good teacher, come home, be a good mom and wife, *and* take time for myself?

The Guardian noted that working intensively over fewer weeks leads to poorer work-life balance and higher stress (Strong, 2019).

Another point: You are meant to spend no more than an hour preparing for each lesson, but to do a half-decent job, you need two hours. Twenty-five hours of lessons a week is already fifty hours. Then marking. *EduTopia* pointed out that chronic emotional exhaustion leaves teachers feeling isolated and less effective (Terada, 2018). When teachers are stressed, relationships with students suffer.

This is what happens when you pour from an empty cup. Eventually, nothing is left to pour.

What can we do, *physically*, to help counter this on a regular basis?

1. Drink water. Dehydration makes everything harder.
2. Eat lunch away from your desk. Even fifteen minutes makes a difference.
3. Step outside once during the day. Fresh air resets something.
4. Laugh with a colleague. Shared laughter is medicine.
5. Leave at contract time at least once a week (but ideally, daily). The work will still be there.

Once you commit to keeping your cup full, or at least not empty, you can look at the bigger picture: your classroom and the students in it. Every generation thinks the upcoming group of kids is a hot mess; that's life, but our current students are different. They have no concept of life before smartphones, social media, or YouTube. They look up answers on YouTube. They are thirsty for knowledge that interests them. Does your classroom reflect that? I am not saying you need a classroom full of technology. Weaving technology into education is vital, but it is not the be-all and end-all. As I've been saying throughout this book, we need to meet our students where they are. We cannot go back to the way students learned before. They are not wired that way. Holding onto the past holds them back and fuels the fire, leading to burnout.

M #3: *Method*

We can work on ourselves internally all day, but if we are not meeting our students where they are, those signs of burnout will remain because of frustration from your students toward you and from you back to them. This cyclical recipe for burnout is resolved with our third M. Our current students cannot learn and comprehend on deeper levels if we teach the same way we taught previous generations. They need to be engaged and have their interests sparked. It is possible in every subject and grade. It just takes some elbow grease and a keen eye.

Keep a clear focus on what you want your classroom environment to be like. Understand that not every lesson will be a home run. Sometimes you will have to go back to the drawing board in the middle of a class period. That is teaching, and it's okay! That doesn't mean this won't work in your classroom. Do you drive a car or ride a bike the same way you did the first time? No. It took practice.

Once I mastered this method and my students understood the expectation, my stress level went down. I connected with each student. I snagged kids falling through the cracks and those who needed more challenge. My classroom naturally differentiated without individualized programs. Yours will, too. This switch is the last step in beating burnout. Once you remember why you are there, keep your cup full, and meet your students where they need to learn, your passion is reinvigorated. The good times start to outweigh the difficult times.

I am not promising every day will be rainbows. That is not possible in any profession, let alone one dealing with children. But being in the classroom will become less stressful and more enjoyable. You will face conflicts as challenges to overcome, not signs that you are not enough.

Because you are enough.

I think back to a troubled sophomore I had, on the brink of failing. He confided that home was an absolute mess. That shift in our relationship made it possible for him to pass. I stuck with him through his high school career. He stumbled multiple times. Then I watched him leave for the Marines because he had finally reached that point.

I think of a quiet freshman. I noticed something off with his work. After developing a relationship, I realized he could not read. He had muddled through school. I stepped in to get him interventions.

I think of a student who was in a very dark place. My students could sign up for computer time during lunch. My lunch coordinated with hers. After a candid conversation, I realized there was more going on inside than she could handle. I helped guide her to assistance.

Each of those students came to me and said thank you. "If it was not for you..."

That is why we do it.

It Is Time to Come Home to Yourself

You have been carrying a lot. The weight of students who are struggling, the pressure of a system that keeps asking for more, the exhaustion that settles into your bones and makes you wonder if you have anything left to give. That weight is real, and you are not weak for feeling it. But the fact that you are still searching, still reading, still hoping for something better tells me everything I need to know about the kind of teacher you are. You have not given up. You are just tired. There is a difference.

Give yourself permission to set down some of that weight. You do not have to fix everything today. You do not have to save every student. You do not have to be perfect. What you do have to do is remember who you are underneath all the burnout and the stress. That good teacher? The one who showed up on day one full of passion and purpose? She is still in there. He is still in there. It is time to come home to yourself. Not next year. Not when things calm down. Now. Because you deserve the same grace you so freely give your students.

The best thing you can do for them is to take care of the person they need most—you. Taking care of yourself is not just about bubble baths and weekend getaways, though those have their place. It is about the daily decisions that either replenish you or further drain you. It is about setting a boundary with that parent who emails at ten o'clock at night and expects an immediate response. It is about leaving the stack of papers on your desk and going home when your contract hours are up, because your family needs you too. It is about saying no to the extra duty so you can say yes to your own sanity.

These are not selfish acts. They are survival acts. They are what allow you to stay in this profession for the long haul without losing yourself in the process. So start small, but start somewhere. One boundary. One no. One decision to protect your peace. That is how you come home to yourself—not in one grand gesture, but in a thousand small choices that add up to a life you are not just surviving, but actually living.

Reflection Questions for this chapter...

When was the last time someone said they were proud of you as a teacher? **When was the last time you said it to yourself?**

Which of the five small things to keep your cup full feels most doable this week? Which feels hardest?

Whose opinion (administrator, parent, colleague, or student) are you carrying that you need to let go of?

Think of a student who is frustrating you right now. Are they *having a hard time, not giving you a hard time?* What might be underneath?

Try This Tomorrow:

Choose one of these strategies to protect your energy:

Strategy	Try This
Write your mission statement	*Spend ten minutes writing why you teach and what you want to accomplish. Put it somewhere you will see it.*
One cup-filling action	*Pick one of the five small things (water, lunch away from the desk, step outside, laugh with a colleague, leave on time). Do it tomorrow.*
One small method shift	*Look at one lesson you are teaching this week. How could you give students one small choice?*
The 5-year perspective	*Ask, "If I look back five years from now, what will I wish I had started changing today?" Write down one answer.*

After trying one of these, jot down one observation. What shifted, even slightly, in your energy or mindset?

CHAPTER 12
PLANNING YOUR TIME, YOUR LESSONS, AND YOUR YEAR

Let's think about the average teacher's life. You wake up before the sun, rush through your morning routine, and barely have time to get your coffee ready before you're out the door. You spend all day on your feet, moving from one thing to the next, answering questions, putting out fires, trying to squeeze in a bathroom break between classes (and potentially, reheat your coffee).

After a full day of this, followed by meetings, coaching, or advising, you finally get home, exhausted, but the work is not done. There are emails to answer, papers to grade, and lessons to plan, let alone what your own family may need from you. You tell yourself you will stop after one more thing, but one more thing turns into two, and before you know it, you are collapsing into bed (or worse, finding yourself waking up at 2 a.m. on the couch), only to do it all over again tomorrow.

We push through the week, telling ourselves summer is coming, but even summer isn't a real break, is it? There are curriculum updates, professional development, classroom prep, and the nagging feeling that you should be doing more.

Sound familiar?

Here's the thing: there's nothing wrong with being wired this way. Most teachers are. We care deeply. We want to help. We don't like saying no. We want to save the world and do everything well, but when that drive gets pushed too far, it stops being a strength and becomes a liability. We give until there is nothing left to give, and that doesn't help anyone.

You have heard me say it before: You cannot pour from an empty cup. Teacher tired is one thing. Burnout is another. The question is, *what can you actually do about it*?

The first step is something called a "time audit." I first heard about this concept at a workshop and honestly thought it sounded ridiculous. "I know what I do," I told myself. "Why do I have to write it down?" But when I finally tried it, I was shocked. I had no idea where my time was actually going.

How to Do a Time Audit

Here's what I want you to do. Pick a day, or a week if you are feeling brave, and write down every single thing you do. I am not talking about a vague to-do list. I am talking about the minute-by-minute, uncomfortable, no-hiding reality of where your time actually goes from the moment you wake up until the moment you go to sleep.

Think of it like keeping a food diary. You know how nutritionists tell you to write down everything you eat? It's because most of us have no idea how many extra calories we are mindlessly consuming. Same idea here. You have no idea how many minutes you are losing to things that do not matter, so write it all down. Scrolling social media for ten minutes? Write it down. A two-minute phone call that could have been a text? Write it down. Fifteen minutes of driving to pick up takeout because you were too exhausted to cook? Write it down. Every single minute you are awake, account for it.

I guarantee you will be shocked at what you find. Do you

have a device that shows your weekly screen time? Have you ever looked at it and thought, "That can't be right"? It is because a little here and a little there adds up in ways we never notice. Five minutes scrolling social media turns into twenty. A "quick" chat with the neighbor while you're grabbing the mail turns into thirty. By the end of the week, you have lost hours to things you cannot even remember doing.

So, what are you looking for? Two things.

First, how productive you actually are. Are you getting a lot of little things done but never finishing the big ones? Or are you crushing the major tasks while the small stuff piles up around you? Neither is wrong, but you need to know which one you are doing.

Second, you are looking for time black holes. You know what I mean. You sit down to look up something quick on Google. Twenty minutes later, you are reading an article about something completely unrelated, watching a video that popped up in your feed, and you cannot remember what you were originally searching for. Those minutes add up faster than anything else.

Once you see it all laid out in black and white, you cannot unsee it. That is the point. This audit is not about making you feel guilty. It is about giving you back control. You do not actually need more hours in the day; you need to know where the hours you have are going and then decide, on purpose, whether they are serving you or stealing from you. Once you know that, you can start making different choices. Not perfect ones. Just better ones.

That is how you stop feeling like there is never enough time.

Breaking Down Your Timing

Now that you know where your time is going, you need

to learn how long things actually take. Not how long you *think* they take. How long do they *actually* take?

Let me give you an example. Grading essays.

If you are anything like me, you probably tell yourself, "I just need a couple of hours," but it never goes as planned. It's really easy to see why once you break it down:

Step	Time
Organize papers and rubrics	*2 minutes*
Read each essay (grammar, spelling, and comments)	*10 minutes*
Fill out the rubric	*3 minutes*
Enter the grade into the gradebook	*2 minutes*

Total per essay: 18 minutes

Now, before you argue with me, I know there are variables. Phone calls. Impromptu meetings. A student stopping by after class. Your own brain decides it needs a break. Those things happen, but even without them, look at the math. Say you have twenty students. Eighteen minutes per essay comes out to approximately six hours.

Six hours.

I used to think grading essays would take two or three hours. Breaking it down this way showed me the truth. No wonder I was always behind. No wonder I felt like I was rushing. I was giving myself half the time I actually needed.

This is where the time suck happens. It's not because we're lazy or bad at our jobs. It's simply because we don't give ourselves enough time, which leads to mental strife, rushing, and mistakes. Then we feel guilty about it, which makes everything worse.

Scheduling It All

Now that you know where your time is going and how long things actually take, it is time to schedule it. I know that sounds obvious, but stick with me. This is not about filling every minute of your day with tasks. This is about finally having a plan you can trust.

First, you need to figure out what kind of planner works for your brain. I am a paper planner person at heart. I love the feel of writing things down, crossing them off, and flipping pages. But for the nitty-gritty timing work, the kind where you move blocks of time around and try to figure out where everything fits, I used Google Calendar. Why? Because it is easy to drag and drop. If something takes longer than expected, you just slide it over. No whiteout. No eraser marks. No rewriting the same task three times.

Once you have your rhythm down and you are not shifting things around as often, you can switch to a paper planner if that is what you prefer. Honestly, use whatever works for you. A basic notebook. A digital app. A desk calendar. The tool does not matter. What matters is that you use it.

Here's what I discovered when I started doing this. We are so used to feeling like we are constantly running behind that we no longer even know what calm feels like. The go-go-go mentality is so ingrained that we think it is just part of the job. But when you actually find out exactly how long something takes and you schedule it into your day or week, something shifts. You stop feeling like you are drowning. You start feeling like you have a handle on things.

You're not constantly worried about the unfinished task because it's no longer living in the back of your mind. You know exactly when you are going to do it. Tomorrow morning. Thursday afternoon. Monday. It's scheduled so your brain can let it go.

Now, let me be real with you. Is it annoying when you do not finish something in the time you allotted? Yes. It is frustrating. You look at the clock, look at your planner, and think, "Well, that didn't go as planned." But here's the thing… There is almost always a reason. You didn't anticipate the task correctly, or an interruption happened, or you were just tired and moving more slowly than usual. That is not a failure. That is data. You adjust and try again. It gets easier with practice. I promise.

Think of it like budgeting money. When you first sit down to create a budget, it can feel overwhelming. You have to look at every dollar coming in and every dollar going out. You have to make hard choices, but once you have a budget in place, everything becomes easier. You know exactly how much you can spend on groceries, on eating out, and on savings. You aren't constantly guessing or hoping it will all work out.

Time is the same way. Once you budget it, you stop feeling frazzled. I used to have Post-its everywhere. Sticky notes on my desk, on my computer monitor, and on the kitchen counter at home. To-do lists that just kept growing. I always felt like I was forgetting something because, honestly, I probably was, but once I got this method down, I wasn't flustered anymore. I knew I had a two-hour window on Tuesday to work on that project. I knew I would answer emails between 3:00 and 3:30 p.m. I knew I would grade those essays on Saturday morning.

Because of this, I started having time for myself. Not because I magically had more hours in the day, but because I stopped wasting the hours I had. I was exercising again. Spending actual quality time with my family. Sitting on the couch without feeling guilty about not working. That is what this does. It doesn't give you more time. It helps you finally see the time you already have, and once you see it, you can use it wisely.

This is the change you have been looking for. Not a magic wand. Not a life overhaul. Just a clear, honest look at where your time goes, and a simple plan to take it back.

Lesson Planning for the Entire Year

Using this concept, let's apply it to the second step of fixing teacher burnout with something that causes more stress for teachers than almost anything else: lesson planning. Not the day-to-day, "What am I teaching tomorrow?" panic, but the bigger picture. The unit pacing. The "Am I going to make it to the end of the curriculum before the test?" dread that lives in the back of your mind from September to May.

When I say, "lesson plan for the year," I don't mean writing out every single activity for every single day. That would be insane, and I would never suggest it, especially since I've been emphasizing that our day-to-day plans should be fluid, based on what is actually happening with our students. What I mean is scheduling yourself out. Mapping the big pieces so you know what is coming, how long you have, and where you might need to adjust. The daily lessons? You fill those in as you go. The framework? That you can do now.

This gives you clarity, less stress, and a sense of calm when a student asks, "What are we doing next week?" or an administrator asks, "Can you show me your pacing?" You aren't guessing. You aren't panicking. You already know.

You can plan your entire year, or if that feels like too much, just start with one month. The goal is to eliminate three things: the rush at the end of the year when you realize you are three weeks behind; the confusion of what is coming next; and the panic of "I need to lesson plan… where am I? How long is this going to take?"

Let me be clear. This is not set in stone. Snow days happen. Fire drills happen. A lesson takes longer than expected, or a student asks a question that sends you down a completely different path. That's all fine. You can move things around, but having a starting point, a map, even if you take detours, is infinitely better than driving blind.

I started doing this when I was student teaching. My cooperating teacher taught me the basic concept, and it was instrumental as I found my own way with it over the years. I wasn't constantly stressed about whether I would make it through the curriculum. I could see the whole picture. I could adjust as I went. Honestly? I never felt the rushed panic that my colleagues did as the days ticked down. It also helped when I was handing out those unit schedules at the beginning of each unit.

The Process

Here is how it works. First, look at your curriculum as a whole. What are the big units? What are the major topics? Again, don't worry about specific activities yet. You aren't planning lessons. You're building a skeleton. The meat comes later.

Step 1: Grab a blank calendar (digital or print, whatever works for you).
Step 2: Fill in the dates for the month(s) you are planning.
Step 3: Mark any school closures, early release days, or schedule changes from your district calendar.
Step 4: Start mapping out your units.

For example, let's say you are teaching World War II:

Topic	**Days to Cover**
War in Europe	*3 days*
Pearl Harbor	*1 day*
Pacific Theater	*3 days*
Home Front	*3 days*
D-Day	*2 days*
Atomic Bombings	*2 days*

This is not permanent. You can rearrange things, but now you know roughly how many days you have for each topic and thus, how many days you need for the unit. When you sit down to plan your actual lessons, you aren't guessing. You know you have three days for the War in Europe. That means you need three activities, or two activities and a review, or whatever fits your vision for that content. The guesswork is gone.

I always physically printed a calendar for the entire school year and worked backward. I started with the last day of school, the very last thing I wanted to cover, and moved backward from there. Week by week. Unit by unit. I color-coded everything. I changed things around constantly. (Again, I am a paper person, so I used a lot of Wite-Out, but you can do this digitally if that is your preference.) By the time I was done, I had a complete map of my year. Did I follow it perfectly? Never. But I had it, and that made all the difference.

The Subconscious Benefit

Here's something you might not expect. Your brain is always spinning in the background. "Will we get through the curriculum? Do we have enough time? What if we fall behind?" Those questions live in the back of your mind, draining energy you don't even realize you are losing. But when you sit down and map out your year, even though you know things will change, your subconscious relaxes. It knows you have a plan. It knows you can adjust. It stops sounding the alarm every five minutes. That is not nothing. That is peace of mind. And peace of mind is something every teacher desperately needs.

Here is one more reason I loved doing this. Inevitably, a student would come up to me and say, "I am going to be out for four days, three weeks from now. What are we going to be covering?" Before I consistently had this map, I would panic. I would dig through my plans, try to figure out where I thought I would be, and hope I was right. After I started mapping my year, I could just look at my calendar and say, "These are the topics we will be covering. Here is what you need to know." I didn't have the specific assignments yet, but I had the framework. That was enough to make a plan for the student, keep them from falling behind, and save me a ton of stress.

This is not about being perfect. It is about being prepared, and being prepared is so much easier than being panicked.

Creating the Individual Lessons

Now that you have your year mapped out, let's talk about what actually goes into each lesson. I know writing lesson plans is tedious. It is probably one of the least favorite parts of the job for most of us, but when you're building a student-centered classroom, objectives aren't just paperwork… they are the backbone of *everything*.

When I first moved to the student-centered model, I kept the same lesson-planning mindset I'd always had. They were just something I had to write down and file away. Once I started really digging into student-centered activities, I realized something: I needed to know exactly what I wanted my students to achieve before I could say whether the lesson was successful. The easiest way to do that? Base the entire lesson around specific, clear objectives that made sense and weren't just bureaucratic fluff.

Over the years, different supervisors have told me that objectives should look different ways. One wanted me to write them based on standards. For example: *"Students will be able to compare and contrast the most important points and key details presented in two texts on the same topic."*

Another wanted an essential question, something broad that the whole lesson would answer. For example: *"Students will be able to answer the question, Was the Renaissance truly a rebirth, or was it actually a whole new baby?"*

Here is what I found works best. Combine the content idea, the core standards, and the essential question into a single objective. For example: *"Students will be able to demonstrate the different points of view of characters in Romeo and Juliet."* That is the sweet spot. It tells you what students need to do, why they are doing it, and how you will know they got there.

Create the objective first, then work backward to figure out how you will get them there. That objective is your North Star. Every activity, every choice board, every discussion question should point back to it. If an activity does not help students meet the objective, it is probably fluff… and you do not have time for fluff.

From here, let's talk about where the actual content of your lessons comes from. In my first year of teaching, my mentor told me something that has stuck with me ever since: No teacher ever needs to completely reinvent the wheel. Of course, sometimes you wake up in the middle of the night with a brilliant idea, and you can't wait to bring it to life. That's great, but most of the time, if you need an idea or just want to jog your thinking, just search for what you're looking for. Chances are, a version of it or exactly what you are picturing already exists. You just need to tweak it for your individual students. Sometimes you stumble across an entire lesson plan with procedures, primary sources, and everything you need.

The goal is not necessarily to buy something. What you find might not be 100 percent student-led, and that's okay. You can always take the basic idea and turn it into a student-centered activity. You can buy a lesson, snag a free one, or, most often, just get a great idea to run with.

Once you have your objectives and your ideas, it is time to put the lesson together. This is where the magic happens.

First, make it engaging. Your students need to be actively involved. Think about what helps them *live* the information, not just fill out a worksheet. Here are a few examples I have seen:

- A math teacher taught percentages through a car-buying simulation. Students had to figure out interest loans, costs, and down payments.
- A health teacher had students do "speed dating" to find compatible partners for a family dynamic project, and he said it worked better than any assigned pairing he had ever tried.
- In social studies, when covering the Great Depression, have students research homelessness today and write letters to local officials comparing the past and present.

Second, give students choice. Offer different assignments. Use a choice board. Give a rubric with somewhat vague instructions, such as "You need to cover X, Y, and Z," but let them determine how to present it. You would be surprised where students take those assignments when you give them free rein. Finally, avoid fluff. Games are great. I am a huge fan of using games in the classroom, but ask yourself, "How is this game proving that students have learned anything?" Make sure they are not just playing. Add an accountability element. Require them to complete a task, answer a question, or demonstrate their knowledge before moving on. They should not just be doing an activity. They should be showing what they learned.

Remember, you don't need to reinvent the wheel. Find what is out there. Adapt it. Make it your own. And always, always start with the objective. That is your North Star. It will guide everything else.

Choosing Yourself Without the Guilt

So where does that leave you? Stuck between a profession that demands everything and a body that is running on fumes. The answer is not to care less. You became a teacher because you care deeply, and that is not something you can just switch off. The answer is to care for yourself with the same intensity you bring to your students. Think about that for a second. You would never look at an exhausted, overwhelmed student and tell them to just push through it. You would tell them to take a break. You would ask what they need. You would make sure they knew it was okay to rest. Yet somehow, you do not extend that same grace to yourself.

It is time to start. Not because self-care is a buzzword or because someone told you to buy more scented candles, but because the way you are operating right now is not sustainable, and deep down, you know it. You cannot keep running on empty and expect to show up as the teacher your students deserve. You cannot keep saying yes to everything and everyone while your own health, your own relationships, and your own sense of self get pushed further and further down the priority list. Something has to change, and that something starts with you giving yourself permission to stop.

Setting boundaries is not selfish. Protecting your time and your energy is not a weakness. It is wisdom, and it is the only way you will still be standing in this profession five, ten, or twenty years from now. You are worth that investment. Start acting like it.

Reflection Questions for this chapter...

What is one "time black hole" you suspect is eating up more of your day than you realize?

What is one unit that always feels rushed? How could working backward help you pace it differently?

What is one teaching task you consistently underestimate the time for?

Think of a time you used an activity that turned out to be fluff. What was missing? How could you add accountability?

Try This Tomorrow:

Choose one of these strategies to try this week:

Strategy	Try This
One-day time audit	*For one day, write down everything you do and how long it takes. Just collect data.*
Break down one task	*Pick a task you have been avoiding. Break it into small steps. Estimate the time for each.*
Schedule one thing	*Put one nonnegotiable personal activity on your calendar this week (a walk, coffee break, or leaving on time). Protect it.*
Map one unit	*Take the next unit. Write down how many days you have. Roughly allocate days to each topic.*
Write a "sweet spot" objective	*Take one lesson. Write an objective combining content, standards, and an essential question.*

After trying one of these, jot down one observation. What surprised you?

CHAPTER 13
THE FORWARD-FACING EDUCATOR

We have covered a lot of ground together.

We started with mindset, shifting how you see your students, your classroom, and yourself. We considered student-centered learning and why the old industrial model no longer fits the students who walk through our doors. We explored student intent, student choice, the flipped classroom, problem-solving, reversing apathy, effective discipline, building relationships, beating burnout, managing your time, and planning lessons that actually work.

That's a lot.

But here is what I want you to remember above all else: You are already a good teacher.

You would not have made it this far if you weren't. You would not have read chapter after chapter about how to better reach your students if you didn't care deeply about doing right by them. The fact that you have stuck with me through thirteen chapters proves your passion for teaching is still alive.

It may be buried under paperwork, behavior issues, and exhaustion. It may be hard to find on some days, but it is there.

The Thread That Runs Through Everything

If there is one idea I hope you carry with you long after you close this book, it is this:

You cannot pour from an empty cup.

Every strategy we have discussed, every choice board, every flipped lesson, every restorative conversation, every time audit, every postcard home, every moment of *aloha*... all of it rests on one foundation: you taking care of yourself first.

Not selfishly. Not lazily. But strategically.

A burned-out teacher cannot save anyone. A stressed-out teacher cannot think creatively. An exhausted teacher cannot see the student who is having a hard time behind the student who is giving them a hard time.

When you pour from an empty cup, everyone suffers... including you. When you keep your cup full, or at least not empty, everything else becomes possible.

Using Snowflakes to Create Your Avalanche

I have said it before, and I will say it again: You cannot fix everything at once, but you can fix things one at a time.

Think of it as snowflakes. No single snowflake feels like much. But snowflake by snowflake, they build into an avalanche.

The same is true in your classroom. You don't need to overhaul everything tomorrow. You don't need to implement all thirteen chapters at once. That would be overwhelming, and overwhelm leads to burnout.

Instead, pick one thing.

- Maybe it's the spirit of *Aloha*... just saying the word to your students tomorrow morning.
- It may be a single postcard to one student who falls through the cracks.

- Maybe it's one questioning technique: "What three things have you already tried?"
- Perhaps it's a two-minute brain break when the energy goes sideways.
- It could be a time audit for one Saturday.
- Maybe it's writing one "sweet spot" objective for a lesson you already teach.

One snowflake. Then another. Then another.

By the end of the school year, you won't recognize your classroom, not because you changed everything overnight, but because you changed one thing at a time, consistently, with intention.

What Now?

You've read this book. Maybe you've highlighted passages. Perhaps you even have dog-eared pages… but you've definitely thought, *I could try that.*

Now it's time to actually try something. Don't let perfectionism paralyze you. Don't wait until you have all the answers. Don't tell yourself, "I'll implement this next year."

Pick one thing. Try it tomorrow. See what happens.

If it flops, tweak it. If it still flops, try something else. If it works, celebrate it… and then add another snowflake.

You aren't alone. There are teachers all over the world facing the same struggles, asking the same questions, trying to figure out how to reach students who seem unreachable. You are part of a community of forward-facing educators who refuse to give up, who refuse to go back to the old ways just because they are comfortable, who refuse to believe that "these kids today" are the problem.

The problem is not the kids. The problem is that the system has not caught up to who they are and how they learn.

But you can catch up. You already are.

One Last Thing

Before you close this book, write down one thing you are going to try tomorrow. Not next week. Not next month. Tomorrow.

It can be small. It can be tiny. It can be as simple as saying, "When you walk in, leave your baggage at the door. You are starting fresh."

Write it down.

Then do it.

Come back to this book when you need a reminder. Mark the pages that spoke to you. Reread the chapters that felt hard. Skip the ones that did not resonate, for now. They might hit differently next year. You have everything you need already inside you. The strategies in this book are just tools to help you access what you already know: that you became a teacher to make a difference, and you still can.

You are a good teacher.
You are enough.
You are not alone.

Now go be the forward-facing educator your students need you to be.

Reflection Questions for this chapter...

Which chapter resonated with you the most? Why?

"You cannot pour from an empty cup." What is one thing you will do this week to fill your own cup?

Which chapter made you the most uncomfortable? What might that discomfort be trying to tell you?

Think of one student who has been hard to reach. What is one small thing you could do differently tomorrow to connect with them?

Don't put this book down without answering this question:

What is the one thing you will do tomorrow?

Write it here: ______________________________

Then do it.

Thank you for reading. Thank you for teaching. Thank you for not giving up.

BIBLIOGRAPHY

Darling-Hammond, L., Friedlaender, D., & Snyder, J. "Student-Centered schools: Policy supports for closing the opportunity gap." *Stanford Center for Opportunity Policy in Education,* 2014. https://learningpolicyinstitute.org/sites/default/files/2024-03/Student_Centered_Learning_SCOPE_CROSS-CASE_POLICY_BRIEF.pdf

Godwin, R. "Work less, live more: Is it time to end the five-day week?" *The Guardian, 2023.* https://www.theguardian.com/society/2023/jan/22/work-less-live-more-is-it-time-to-end-the-five-day-week

Klein, R. "American teachers feel really stressed, and it's probably affecting students." *Huffpost,* 2014. https://www.huffpost.com/entry/gallup-education-report_n_5119966

Strong, W. "Work isn't working – but a four-day week would help fix it." *The Guardian,* 2019. https://www.theguardian.com/commentisfree/2019/feb/01/work-four-day-week-workloads-stress-economy

Terada, Y. "Burnout isn't inevitable. Teachers are stressed—but schools can help." *EduTopia,* 2018. https://www.edutopia.org/article/burnout-isnt-inevitable/

...and, of course, if you would like to learn more from me at Student-Centered World, visit www.studentcenteredworld.com

ABOUT THE AUTHOR

Jenn Breisacher started teaching high school history in 2007. Like most new teachers, she was told to stand at the front of the room and lecture. Spoiler Alert: It didn't work. When her school mandated student-centered learning with no training, most of her early attempts failed...but the successes showed her she was onto something real.

She kept experimenting, teaching in two very different New Jersey schools: a competitive academic high school and a Title I CTE school. The same strategies worked in both because the problem was never the kids; it was the system. After five years of trial and error, she built a student-centered framework that worked consistently for nearly every student.

In 2018, she founded Student-Centered World, where she has been teaching other teachers how to apply this framework. She has since worked with teachers in 18 countries, has been featured in Business Insider, and has built a community of forward-facing educators who refuse to give up on their students or themselves.

Jenn lives in coastal North Carolina with her husband, two children, and two dogs. When not writing or coaching teachers, she's on the water, at a sports field, or camping with her family.

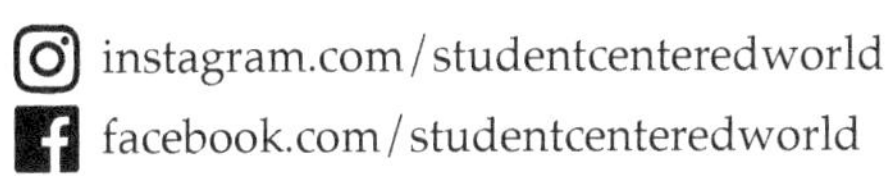

ACKNOWLEDGMENTS

In 2018, I had a crazy idea. I loved giving workshops on my teaching style, and my co-workers started encouraging me to do something bigger. This was pre-2020, so building a whole business online was still seen as risky and "not a real job". I remember when I got my master's online, a few people asked me if it was even a real degree, so I knew what I was up against. I ran the idea past my husband, Shawn, and without hesitation, he helped me jump in headfirst. Student-Centered World was born.

Since then, he and my children have watched me have the highest of highs and the lowest of lows as the field of education has changed just as much as what I do every day. My boys have learned the tenacity required to be an entrepreneur and also a present parent. Putting this book together is a dedication to them and their constant encouragement of their "teacher teacher" mom. Thanks, guys, for being my why.

Go fast, turn left.

In terms of this book, thanks to my editor, Ita, who helped craft an overflow of ideas into an actual book; my proofreader, Ashi, who polished it; and Carin and the artistic team, who took my vision and made it into an amazing cover. Without your help, none of this would have come to fruition.

I wish I could name all the teachers I have worked with over the years as you all have taught me as much as I've taught you, but I especially want to shout out those who helped me with this book: Keanon Lewis, David Mendenhall, Nicholas Chizek, Jenna Schuld, Araceli Calle, Maria Donadie M. Viernes, PhD, Emily Merian, Suzie Morris, Tiffany Turner Surles, Meghan Koellner, Johanna Rowland, Elizabeth Colbert, Marcus Manow, Robin Linehan, Robin Gant, Rocio Gonzalez Bendiksen, Eilene Weimar, Abigail Myers, and everyone else who participated.

Lastly, thanks to everyone I have worked with over the years, from John, who took a chance on me in 2007, Danielle, who gave me the space to really go out on a limb and hone in on this model in 2013, and Bridget and Drew, because obviously.

To my former students, I separate you into two categories: the ones who (begrudgingly) put up with me as I found my own way with student-centered learning (again, many apologies for those early years), and those who kept me on my toes as much as I kept you on yours in those later years. I'm proud of the people you are turning into, and that I could be one short blip in your own stories. Keep following your hearts and stay curious.

www.ingramcontent.com/pod-product-compliance
Ingram Content Group UK Ltd.
Pitfield, Milton Keynes, MK11 3LW, UK
UKHW062308290726
14090UKWH00018B/951